CHILDREN OF POVERTY

Studies on the Effects of Single Parenthood, the Feminization of Poverty, and Homelessness

edited by

STUART BRUCHEY
University of Maine

A GARLAND SERIES

Contents

Tables

Figures

Acknowledgments

Most people who are acknowledged in books are rather privileged and rarely in need of special mention. They are the spouses, family, friends, and associates of the authors who may have experienced some inconveniences along the way but usually have not endured the slings and arrows which life throws at the poor, the battered, the homeless, and the hungry. While we recognize and thank those around us who have helped with the production of this book, we know they understand who really are in need of recognition, acknowledgment, and support.

We dedicate this study to the boys and girls for whom Hopeful Horizons was conceived, planned, and implemented. It is to the hundreds who were helped that we devote our attention, and sadly, it is to the hundreds or thousands who were not helped that we owe both special recognitions and regrets.

To Rex, who seemed confident as he wrote:

> When I was a kid, I did not have a father. I had to learn everything by myself. I learned how to ride a bike by myself. When I was 7 I got a father but he smoked coke. So he beat us over every little thing. I had to run away once. But now I'm 14 and I'm a good kid and I'm doing pretty good. I'm going to school. I have a roof over my head and food in my mouth. When I grow up I want a good life for my kids. I want to be a lawyer. I won't beat my kids.

To Charles, who sounds like a survivor:

> My father is a butthole, who is very ignorant, and my mother is a very considerate person, which is very awesome. If you ask me, they spend too much time trying to stay away from each other.
> There are three things that I will NOT do when I grow up. These are: I will not cheat on my girlfriend; beat on my kids; or leave them alone by themselves.

To Jack, whose poetry we shared:

> I am a small spider aloof by the bay,
> my legs are now weary,
> my friends are all gay (happy).
> I am a small spider, I'm hungry, yes sir.
> I try to stop thinking, about hunger,
> but look! Feast your eyes on her,
> She is a small fly all fluttering by,
> she looks so wonderful,
> with wings shade of gold,
> her eyes are pink,
> who knows what they hold,
> but now I'm still right here all alone,
> a small little spider aloof in the cold.

To Amy, whose cry was heard:

> I cry when I fight with you.
> I cry when I talk with you.
> I cry when I miss you.
> I cry when I think of you.
> I cry.

To Niah, whose cry may not have been heard,

> I am lonely
> Forever in a day.
> No one sees or hears.
> I talk but who really listens?
> I'm out here alone.
> Or, at least that's how it seems.
> Or, am I alone?

And, belatedly, we acknowledge Chad who had won 1st prize in a poster contest and proudly posed for a picture beneath two banners which read, "Fulfill the Dream" and "Practice Nonviolence." We say belatedly, because Chad was killed at age 14 as he jumped from a speeding stolen car being driven by a 13 year old friend.

To these young Americans, who may or may not fulfill their dreams, who may or may not grow up to practice nonviolence, who may or may not grow up at all, we dedicate this study of one attempt to make a difference in their lives.

K. Lively
Paul F. Kleine
June 10, 1996

The School as a Tool for Survival for Homeless Children

I

Introduction

"When you have to live in one room with your whole family and take care of the kids while your mom does whatever she's doing, you just don't have your homework done." This quotation is a window into the world of a homeless child which reveals circumstances that may produce alienation. While other young people are trying to decide which popular name brand tennis shoes to buy, many homeless youth are concerned with how to hold their families together.

Who are the homeless children and where do they come from? "Street waifs," or "street children," as they were called in the 1800's are today's homeless children; 500,000 reported in 1987 by the National Coalition for the Homeless (Ely, et al., 1987). Families that include school age children are without jobs, without shelter, without food, and wandering the streets in city after city. They are families that come from many walks of life. One family, convinced of imminent danger, left Missouri to escape a much publicized earthquake that never took place. This once stable family of seven joined the ranks of the homeless. The ambitions immediately changed from long-term to short-term; plans for home ownership, education and retirement transformed into worries about food, shelter, and employment.

And then there was Maria, one of the growing number of children bearing children: a 15-year-old with a 9-month-old baby and expecting a second soon. Because her family had rejected her, she was living in a shelter. She had a primary need of day care for her child because of her desire to continue her education at the transitional site for the homeless. Others living in the shelter were like Randal, whose mother had taken him and left the home they were sharing with a man who had become physically abusive. Randal, who had always been an excellent student, exceeded the number of absent days allowed by the public school. When told he would be retained next year, he began losing the motivation to perform academically. These and many more like them are children in need.

How is the demand to educate the homeless children being answered? With the passing of The Stewart B. McKinney Homeless Assistance Act (P.L. 100-77) in July 1987, many states have initiated efforts to address the issues of educating the homeless student. This has presented several areas of concern to the established school districts and its tenacious attitude toward policies. In the report of the National Coalition for the Homeless, Ely, et al. (1987) found long-standing rules requiring documents of immunization, residency, etc. are perpetuated within the schools, the homeless children come without these required documents and are often turned away. Other studies found many homeless children were not attending school.

> A survey completed by the Child Welfare League of America found that 43% of homeless children were not enrolled in any school program. In numbers, this translates into 4 out of every 10 homeless children of school age not attending any school. . . . the children who go to school are often met with jeers, taunts and rejection (Eddowes & Hranitz, 1989, p. 198).

In investigating how homeless people are defined, the National Coalition for the Homeless (1989) outlined The McKinney Act definition for the homeless as: "lacking a fixed, regular and adequate nighttime residence, living in shelters, institutions (other than a prison) or any facility not designed or used for a sleeping accommodation for human beings" (p. 2). The McKinney Act further stated the conditions of provision for educating homeless children (National Coalition for the Homeless, 1989). Each state will receive funding contingent to fulfillment of the following plan:

> Each state must adopt a plan to provide for the education of homeless children and to provide procedures to resolve disputes regarding the educational placement of homeless children. In addition, each plan must ensure, to the extent practical under local education laws, that: (a) local education

> authorities continue the education of the child in the original school district for the rest of the school year or place the child in the district he is actually living in, whichever is in the child's best interest; (b) each homeless child is provided the same services as other children; (c) the records of each homeless child who is transferred to a new school district are available in that district in a timely manner (p. 18).

In regard to the potential hindrances of the homeless children to receiving an education, each state will adopt the following policy:

> Each state education agency must ensure that homeless children have access to free and appropriate public school education and that state residence requirements do not bar access (National Coalition for the Homeless, 1989, p. 17).

When investigating the rationale for denying homeless children an education, Ely, et al. (1987) found numerous excuses. "In some cases, school districts deliberately exclude homeless children from their classroom. In other cases, denial is caused by ignorance and inflexibility" (p. 4).

Flexibility and creativity are suggested as means to assist in providing an equal opportunity education (Ely, et al., 1987; Life, 1990). Many states are attempting to be flexible by providing on-site locations at shelters for educating the homeless. Others are developing new policies to determine who is responsible for the costs of educating the homeless child (National Coalition for the Homeless, 1989). In the area of creativity, a computerized tracking system is being contemplated by several states, which would identify school-age children in shelters and hotels to ascertain previous enrollment and expedite current enrollment. Others outside the educational system have devised creative ways of teaching photography to homeless children. Jim Hubbard, a photojournalist from Washington D.C., has been interviewed by the media telling his story of teaching the homeless children to photograph themselves. The results are described as expressions of joy and love in an otherwise derogatory situation (Life, 1990).

City Park School of Dallas attributed their successful attempt at flexibility and creativity in educating the homeless children to three factors:

(a)the orientation of students

(b)a coordinated effort by the entire staff

(c)active involvement of community groups (Gonzalez, 1990, p. 785-786).

The orientation consisted of an introduction of children and parents to the principal who discussed the rules and incentives for academic and behavioral achievement. All supplies are provided and the child is walked to class, introduced and given a warm welcome. Each child is then assigned a buddy, appointed to be seen twice a week by a counselor, and seen by a nurse.

The coordinated efforts by the staff include an emphasis on learning basic skills. In placing a student in a classroom, learning styles are matched with teaching styles. Weekly staff meetings are held to identify the students needing extra help and they are tutored before and after school. The staff members act as a liaison between the parents, medical, and social agencies that assist with services.

Community agencies have provided funding for books, school supplies, and items from the wish lists of needed items in individual classrooms. Many of the groups provide parent workshops, classroom volunteers, and after-school recreational activities.

Probably the most supportive aspect of this school is its underlying philosophy which is ". . . when homeless students attend school, it is the responsibility of the school to establish a climate of sharing, caring, and learning. A sense of 'family' is what these children chiefly need" (Gonzalez, 1990, p. 787). City Park reported scores at a high level of mastery on the criterion-referenced test required by the state of Texas (Gonzalez, 1990).

Oklahoma also has begun to face the challenge of educating the homeless children. In a regional summary report on the shelters serving homeless children, the Oklahoma State Department of Education (1989) concluded that collectively 10 shelters within Morgan County served a total of 882 school-age children. (Names of persons and places have been changed throughout this study to provide anonymity to the participants.) Of the 882 children served, 48% were not enrolled in any school. The Oklahoma newspapers portrayed the reaction of the state: "400 children living in parks and campgrounds," (Perry, 1990); "cold weather drives homeless families into the shelters," (Homeless Students, 1990); and "alarmed by the statistics" (Smith, 1991).

STATEMENT OF THE PROBLEM

At its broadest level, this study examined the development and implementation of a program designed to serve the educational needs of homeless children in Morgan County. More concretely, the day-to-day activities and perceptions of the administrators, staff, and students of a program called Hopeful Horizons were studied to observe the dynamic changes in the evolution of the program. Attention was focused on the external systems which impinge on the program as well as the characteristics of the homeless children and their perceptions of themselves and their families in the context of being homeless. This analytical description sought a better understanding of the problem of attending to the educational needs of homeless children of school age rather than an evaluation of the success or failure of Hopeful Horizons to educate homeless children.

RESEARCH STUDY CONTEXT

Evolution of the Program

With the increase of unemployment due to the oil crisis and other aspects of the recession that have depressed the economy in Oklahoma, this state joins the national ranks with the number of homeless families growing. Many states have tried to absorb the homeless school-age children directly into the school setting while others have chosen to maintain a separate facility or alternative school.

Initially it appeared that this program had begun in a separate facility on November 6, 1990 with a grant of $200,000 received by the Morgan County School District from the federal funds provided through the Stewart B. McKinney Homeless Assistance Act. However, in January 1991, after interviewing several staff members, it was apparent that the center had a prior history. Evidently, two citizens connected with community agencies had met several times informally discussing “a vision” of starting a school that would teach only students whose families were homeless. How this program evolved from a charitable community effort to a small unit of .3% of the projected 1990-1991 total membership within the Morgan County School District was subsequently explored.

Current Program

The homeless school-age children who served as the focus of this study were in a program funded through the Morgan County Public School District by the federal government in cooperation with a coalition of several community service organizations. Hopeful Horizons is a small school located in the Community Center of Morgan County. This center for homeless children is the newest member of the 18 alternative education facilities operating within the district. It comprises approximately 6% of the total number of students in 1990-1991 alternative facilities and has an average daily membership of 15 transported from various shelters in the county.

Hopeful Horizons is operated by the district in conjunction with the Board of Community Agencies which meets monthly. The board represents 25 community agencies around the city. Those agencies include shelters, charitable organizations, and private businesses. The board raises funds to supplement the McKinney Funds distributed through the school district by the federal government. One representative from the school district also sits in on the board meetings to represent the school’s interest. The school administrative representative returns to the school with the concerns of the community agencies. In cooperation, the school district and community agencies hired the staff of Hopeful Horizons.

The program staff consists of: the program director, social worker, two teachers, a half-time speech and language pathologist, a secretary, and several volunteers. Currently, half of the salary of the director of Hopeful Horizons derives from the federal funds channeled through the district and half from one of the community agencies. All other salaries and expenses are derived from the federal funding; however, the charities have donated many furniture items and supplies. The center occupies part of the first level of the two-story building housing the Community Center.

There are two adjacent offices for the director and secretary and one separate office shared by the social worker and speech and language pathologist.

One open classroom contains the two teachers, volunteers, all the students and a media center. The teachers divide the students according to the "younger" and "older"; younger being kindergarten through second or third grades and older being third or fourth grades through high school. The division of younger and older is decided daily due to the unpredictability of attendance. The students are divided according to several factors: age, ability of the student to attend to the lesson, and number of students present that day. The kitchen, rest room facilities, conference room and an assembly room used for student activities are shared with other groups that the Community Center coordinates.

Food is brought in by the Morgan County District with breakfast and lunch provided. The center keeps the same school calendar as the district schools. School operates daily Monday through Friday from 8:30 a.m. to 3:00 p.m.

Homeless Children of School Age

All homeless children were transported by a community agency from the shelters to the center. The students enrolling in the program in February, 1991 and staying at least five days were included in the sample population. These students received the psychological screening. The manpower was not available to screen all students. February, the coldest month of the year, was chosen as it offered the highest enrollment. Enrollment fluctuated somewhat, with 28 enrolled in February; 9 did not stay over 5 days, 3 did not participate, but 16 were included in the sample. Ten families were represented by the 16 students: 7 males, 9 females, 1 American Indian, 8 Blacks, 5 Caucasians and 2 Hispanics, ranging from 5 years to 16 years of age. The only limitation to including students in the sample, other than length of stay, was obtaining permission from parents who did not want to divulge information about themselves or their children for fear their location may be found out, e.g. an abusive spouse making threats. The parents of three children representing two families declined.

Shelters

In an initial survey of shelters, it was found that approximately 10 different shelters around Morgan County participated in transporting the children to the transitional center. The shelters provided services including emergency assistance for shelter, food, victims of alcohol and drug abuse, medical attention, and clothing. The average length of stay is 30 days in a shelter; therefore, Hopeful Horizons attempted to place the student in the regular school setting within that period of time.

Role of the Researcher

Working under the auspices of the Morgan County Public School District, the senior author became a participant-observer when joining the team selected to evaluate the transitional program for the homeless children. Formally involved as part of the team, she was then allowed the opportunity to conduct research. The involvement required 8 to 24 hours a week from January through November 1991. Although the evaluation process began in November of 1990, direct involvement for the purpose of research was delayed by site relocation. The director had indicated a need for psychological screenings. She explained that many had apparent emotional difficulty and were hard to control. Knowing which students to refer to the special education department for a complete psychological battery was considered valuable information for the success of the students and the program. The senior author was allowed to conduct screenings in February. A comprehensive report, a staff conference, and a parent conference to discuss test results were conducted. After February, only the severe acting students were tested by a retired school psychologist for Morgan County. Formal observations, interviews, surveys, board meetings, special events, testing students, report writing, and parent conferences were held at the program site. Time was spent with staff members and students toward gaining their acceptance.

RESEARCH OBJECTIVES

The following research objectives were investigated in this study to enhance the education of homeless children. The objectives were:

1.To describe the evolution of Hopeful Horizons as a response to educating homeless children.

2.To describe the perceptions of motivation, success in school, anxiety, depression, helplessness, and family-life of the homeless children.

DEFINITION OF TERMS

Ecology of Human Development. The ecology of human development involves the scientific study of the progressive, mutual accommodation between an active, growing human being and the changing properties of the immediate settings in which the developing person lives, as this process is affected by relations between these settings, and by the large contexts in which the settings are embedded (Bronfenbrenner, 1979, p. 21). This model of ecology allows the investigator to view the homeless children and youth within the context of each setting that influences their lives beginning with the most direct influence and expanding to the most indirect influence.

Expectation. Expectation is the cognitive representation of the contingency of response to outcome (Seligman, 1975).

Homeless Person. A person who (1) lacks a fixed, regular and adequate nighttime residence, or (2) lives in (a) a shelter, (b) an institution (other than a prison), or (c) a place not designed for or ordinarily used as a sleeping accommodation for human beings (National Coalition for the Homeless, 1989, p. 2).

Setting. A setting is a place where people can readily engage in interpersonal interaction--home, day care center, playground, etc. (Bronfenbrenner, 1979, p. 22).

THEORETICAL FRAMEWORK

This research is an effort to analyze and describe both the person and the environment as critical determinants of behavior. Two theoretical frameworks, one of an ecological and one of a psychological perspective, are used as models. An ecological theory permits investigation of the systems within the ecology of the homeless child and how those systems influence the evolution of an educational program designed to meet the needs of homeless children. A psychological theory of helplessness provides a framework by which to view the perceptions of the homeless children. Thereby the issue of educating them may be conceptualized by both a broad ecological and narrow individualized or psychological view in an effort to explain the process of educating homeless children of school age.

Ecological Perspective

Urie Bronfenbrenner (1979) suggested investigations must include the systems in which individuals are encompassed in their environment. The interrelations of these systems directly and indirectly determine the extent of "psychological growth" of the individual. These "interconnections" between and within the systems can be either supportive or destructive to the developing person. Also the significant individuals within each setting who interact with each other have an indirect but definite effect on the child's development. The systems can be viewed as layers of the environment graphically demonstrated in Figure 1-1.

Within the context of homelessness beginning at the broadest level, relationships in the ecological environment are observed. Observations at deeper levels of complexity allow a more complete analysis of data when viewing homeless children within an educational setting. The outer most layer is the macrosystem, which according to Bronfenbrenner (1979),

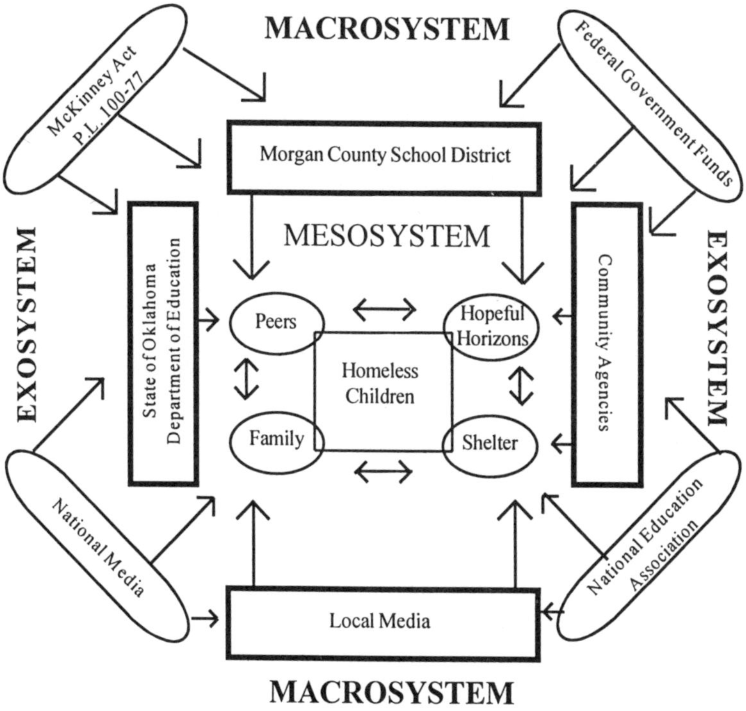

Figure 1-1. The ecological systems adapted to Bronfenbrenner's Model of Ecology (1979) which influence homeless children.

> . . . refers to consistencies, in the form and content of lower-order systems (micro-, meso-, and exo-) that exist, or could exist, at the level of the subculture or the culture as a whole, along with any belief systems or ideology underlying such consistencies (p. 26).

The macrosystem of the homeless child consists of the National Education Association, the national media, the McKinney Act, and federal funds. The National Education Association advocates that every child should have the basic determinants of life, i.e. food, clothing, shelter. This prevailing value has had a significant impact as the media on a national level has revealed the disturbing issue of the rising homelessness of school-age children across the nation. There has been a blitz of media coverage on the causes of and probable solutions to the growing problem of homelessness facing our society today. This compelled legislators to pass the McKinney Homeless Assistance Act (P.L. 100-77). This law included a commitment from the federal government to supply funds to states that respond to the growing concern of the education of the homeless children. Thereby each of these systems has impacted the educational process of the homeless child.

The macrosystem has a direct link to the next layer of the environment, the exosystem, which according to Bronfenbrenner (1979), ". . . refers to one or more settings that do not involve the developing person as an active participant, but in which events occur that affect, or are affected by, what happens in the setting containing the developing person" (p. 25). The exosystem has an even stronger influence on the developing person. The decisions made in several if not all of the settings within this system have a direct application to the present and future of the individual. This system may also either impoverish or enhance development and includes community agencies, the State of Oklahoma Department of Education, the Morgan County Public School District, and the local media.

In Oklahoma, the community agencies within Morgan County had already begun to formulate Hopeful Horizons, an educational center for homeless children. Simultaneously, the State of Oklahoma Department of Education set up a position to receive the McKinney Funds for which the Morgan County Public School District had written a proposal, amounting to a $200,000 federal grant. The local media spotlighted the Hopeful Horizons Center encouraging community involvement. The community agencies and the district became the main decision makers concerning the program.

The next environmental layer is the mesosystem which, according to Bronfenbrenner (1979), ". . . comprises the interrelations among two or more settings in which the developing person actively participates (such as, for a child, the relations among home, school, and neighborhood peer group; for an adult, among family, work, and social life)" (p. 25).

The mesosystem within the environment of homeless children consists of their peers, family, shelter, and the Hopeful Horizons Center where the children are educated. All of these forces influence the homeless child almost daily. Within the mesosystem, the relationships in the microsystem (the final system) have an even greater power to enhance or deplete the developing person. The interactions are direct at certain times and form meaningful linkages between microsystems, as when child and parent move into the shelter or when a social worker from the center visits child and parent at the shelter.

The final layer or core of the environment of the homeless child in different settings constitutes the microsystem which, according to Bronfenbrenner (1979), ". . . is a pattern of activities, roles, and interpersonal relations experienced by the developing person in a given setting with particular physical and material characteristics" (p. 22).

The several microsystems of child with parent, child with peer, child in center, or child in shelter contain many meaningful relationships. The microsystem of greatest concentration for this research is the homeless child in the Hopeful Horizons Center; however, the other settings have also been investigated to some degree in this study. The definition of the microsystem is given a phenomenological emphasis to include the child's perceptions as well as the objective properties of the environment. Most outside influences that affect the developing person cannot be adequately described objectively. The aspects of the environment that powerfully determine the "psychological growth" of the person are those that have personal meaning to the developing person in that particular setting (Bronfenbrenner, 1979).

Psychological Perspective

In viewing the microsystem of homeless children in an educational setting, the emotional aspects of the child must also be investigated. Seligman (1975) stated that helplessness is produced by events seen as uncontrollable. The helplessness then disrupts the ability of the child to learn. Hartman (1989), Tower and White (1989), Ploeg (1989), Eddowes and Hranitz (1989), and others used the term "helplessness" to describe the homeless.

Bassuk (1987) tested 156 homeless children and reported that:

> . . . a majority of the children were suffering from serious emotional problems. Using a childhood depression scale, we found that of the children older than 5, 51% were depressed . . . most had suicidal thoughts . . . 60% manifested intense anxiety. High levels of depression and anxiety certainly interfere with the capacity to learn . . . 54% had repeated a grade and 29% were in special classes (p. 22).

The unpredictability and uncontrollability of the homeless child's life situations may produce the lack of motivation, depressed cognitive perceptions, and emotional tendency toward depression and anxiety that appear to be typical of their behavior. In a behavioral-cognitive theory of helplessness, Seligman (1975) depicted the uncontrollable situations in a person's life as causing three types of disruptions:

(a)the motivation to respond is sapped; diminished initiation of responding to control the outcome

(b)the ability to perceive success is undermined; difficulty at learning that responding succeeds

(c)emotionality is heightened; heightened anxiety followed by depression (p. 44).

There are three basic components to the theory. First, the person has information about the contingency of outcome on the response. The developing children would learn that there is no connection between any response to change their situation of homelessness and the outcome. Then the contingency is transformed into a cognitive representation or expectation of the contingency. The homeless children would learn that relief is independent of their response to being homeless; therefore, the expectation of relief is negated. This then becomes the causal condition for the motivational, cognitive, and emotional debilitation that occurs with helplessness (Seligman, 1975). This suggests that if homelessness continues, the children may no longer expect escape. They could become conditioned to accept homelessness, which may perpetuate helplessness.

Considering the conditions of the motivation, cognition, and emotions that impede learning, it becomes even more difficult to design an educational program for homeless children. The task is then set before the school to educate students with the least amount of humiliation and stigmatization while providing the best possible education which is their right to receive. In a special issue on homelessness, The American Psychologist (1991) published articles emphasizing the use of an ecological theory in providing a framework to view the environment of the homeless. Learned helplessness among other theories was presented as a theory to assist in understanding the effects of homelessness on the individual. In this issue, Toro, Trickett, Wall, and Salem (1991) present a discussion of the ecology of the homeless. Several models are offered for use in viewing the interactions of the environmental systems influencing the homeless individual. Researchers investigating homelessness are encouraged to assess their data at these multiple levels to assist in understanding the complexities of being homeless. Goodman, Saxe, and Harvey (1991) discuss the potential of an emotional disorder as a result of being homeless. Learned helplessness and social disaffiliation are suggested as constructs which may be used by investigators to interpret the trauma to the individual who is homeless. One article in this same journal on homelessness alludes to the school as a significant influence in the educational lives of the homeless children. However, research depicting the attempts at educating these children is not represented (Rosenberg, Solarz, & Bailey, 1991).

II

Review of the Literature

OVERVIEW OF EDUCATING HOMELESS CHILDREN

In the 1850's in St. Louis, a movement known as Travelers Aid began and has to this date been associated with the homeless. Hall and Maza (1990) reported that being alarmed by the increases in the homeless families served, Travelers Aid and the Child Welfare League of America joined forces to research 404 single homeless individuals and 163 families across the nation. Of the 340 children in the study, the average age was six years old and 43% of the school-age children were not currently attending a school. The children attending a school were in local schools with the exception of one city that had a school at the shelter. It was reported that the children felt stigmatized as "kids from the shelter" and felt ashamed and embarrassed. They were believed to be at risk, physically and psychologically, by health care professionals.

First and Cooper (1989) reported that after the first hearing on homelessness held since the Depression, the sum of $100 million was appropriated by the 1983 Congress. With this appropriation, local governments began allocating funds to assist with emergency housing for the homeless. In 1985, Congress mandated investigation of homelessness, and in 1987 the Stewart B. McKinney Homeless Assistance Act was signed into law and appropriated $1 billion for emergency assistance for the homeless. This law also provides access to education (42 U.S.C. Sections 11431-11435).

> 1.Each state educational agency shall assure that each child of a homeless person and homeless youth shall have access to a free

appropriate public education, which would be provided to the children of a resident of the state.

2.Each state that has a residency requirement for school attendance purposes shall review and revise such laws to assure that such children are afforded a free and appropriate public education.

3.Each state shall establish or designate an Office of Coordinator of Education of Homeless Children and Youth. This Office shall gather data on homeless children in the state and develop a plan providing for their education.

4.The plan developed shall contain provisions designed to authorize the state educational agency, the local education agency, the parent or guardian of the homeless child, the homeless youth, or the applicable determinations required. The plan also shall provide procedures for the resolution of disputes regarding the educational placement of these children.

5.Under the plan, the local education agency of each homeless child shall either continue the child's enrollment in the school district of origin for the remainder of the year or enroll the child in the school district where he or she is living, whichever is in the child's best interests.

6.Each homeless child shall be provided services comparable to the services provided to other students in the school being attended.

7.The educational records of each homeless child or youth shall be maintained so that the records are available in a timely fashion. In addition to creating a uniform policy to guarantee access to education for homeless children, the McKinney Act also provides funds to states to develop programs to serve the special needs of homeless children (First and Cooper, 1989, p. 762-763).

The National Academy of Sciences report of 1988 stated the phenomenon of homeless children was a national disgrace which demanded an urgent response. Most of the funds have been appropriated for housing. However, the psychological difficulties have prevented these families from maintaining a stable home (Lauriat, 1986).

> There is a belief that family homelessness has been caused exclusively by external factors such as the

> shortage of low-income housing, the inadequacy of AFDC benefits, and the breakdown of family structure in association with poverty. Our data suggest that psychosocial factors, particularly family breakdown, play an important role as well (Bassuk, Rubin, & Lauriat, 1986, p. 1100).

In Philadelphia, the majority of the 100 families studied by the United Way were "single-mother-headed households" and 31.3% reported leaving home to avoid battering by a spouse (Fox & Roth, 1989, p. 146). In a study of homeless women in the Detroit area that included 165 children, Mills and Ota (1989) concluded that "when available resources fail to prevent homelessness among families, programs and policies should focus on saving the children . . . educational programs that emphasize skill development and esteem building must be made available" (p. 488).

Harrington-Lueker (1989a) reported that 500,000 children, of which 220,000 are school age, are known to live in cardboard boxes, welfare hotels, cars, or under overpasses in the U.S. With the rise of homelessness, educating these children becomes a difficult problem. Rosenman and Stein (1990) reported one obstacle to enrollment in a public school for the homeless was the temporary residence or shelter being located outside district boundaries. They further suggested that school officials must assist shelters in encouraging parents to send their children to school and in providing tutoring at the shelter. In another description of homelessness, Harrington-Lueker (1989b) listed other problems schools must confront: "increased transportation costs, high turnover rates, no address for the registration form, no emergency telephone number where the parent can be reached, no income, and therefore no tax dollars for the school coffers" (p. 13-14).

In a report by the National Coalition for the Homeless (Ely, et al., 1987), the denial of education is brought about by residency requirements, lack of transportation, lack of records, special education requirements, and guardianship requirements. The report not only implied that education can assist the homeless child but stated explicitly:

> For a homeless child, education offers probably the only road out of his seemingly hopeless situation. It offers contact with a stable, sheltered world; it provides examples of strength and courage; it teaches self-worth

> and initiative. And it provides badly-needed skills (p. 21).

School districts have had diverse reactions to the challenge posed by the homeless needing education. Some have taken the challenge to heart, applied for the McKinney Funds and started programs responding to this growing need. The New Jersey State Department of Education received a $129,000 grant and began revision of the policies that act as barriers to allowing the homeless children into the schools (Shelly, 1988).

In Utah, Salt Lake City began a separate classroom on the shelter premises which offers individualized education with no barriers. Similar programs exist in San Diego, California, and Santa Clara, California. New York City devised an elaborate plan of tracking homeless children by computer in an effort to have the former school responsible for the cost of education (Ely, et al., 1987).

New York was able to alter its residency requirements to allow a choice of school district by the parents of homeless children. Maine accepted McKinney Funds to develop their plan to assure access to education for the homeless children. Connecticut law states that the former district will pay the sheltering district the cost of education and transportation of the homeless children. McKinney Funds were received by Washington state to install a computer for tracking purposes (First & Cooper, 1989). In Texas, Houston's district opened two residential schools but for legal purposes was only allowed to keep the service open until 9:00 p.m. However, Joan Raymond, the superintendent stated, "We raised the level of consciousness" of the public concerning homeless children (Penning, 1989, p. 25).

In Dallas, the City Park School mentioned earlier was chosen as one of the 15 exemplary programs in the nation which has 30% of the children coming from condemned apartment buildings or shelters (Gonzalez, 1990). The principal in southwest Queens of New York City may owe his success of integrating the homeless children into the school to his personal belief of how to view them. "Forget the bureaucratic monitoring and artificial distinctions between 'hotel kids' and 'regular kids.' We serve children with or without labels" (Quinn, 1989, p. 18). In California, Orange County received McKinney Funds and began a "classroom on wheels," which contains computers, as well other aids to learning, installed in a motor home (Balfour, 1991, p. 31).

Balfour (1991) also gave Project H.O.P.E. (Homeless Outreach Project for Education) credit for assisting in the educational process by sending credentialed teachers to parks, motels, etc. where the children are living. The areas of assistance include tutoring, academic assessment, parental counseling, record review, and referral to other agencies. The newsletter published by the National Coalition for the Homeless (1991) reported the recommendations of the Senate Appropriations Committee to the full Senate on FY1992 funding. The expanded Education Grants for Homeless Children program received a significant increase over FY1991 from $7.4 to $25 million in the Senate.

ECOLOGICAL ORIENTATION TO EDUCATING HOMELESS CHILDREN

When exploring educating the homeless, as Bronfenbrenner (1977) found, a variety of factors come into play from several different settings. It would not be appropriate or even feasible to take all the homeless children from their families and present environments in order to educate them. Therefore, they must be viewed in the context of each of the significant settings which directly interconnect: family, peers, shelter, and educational center. Then the indirect interconnections that also influence the homeless child must be considered: the community agencies, school administrators of the district, department of education within the state, and local media. Finally, the "consistencies," e.g. the federal government, laws passed, national media, and any cultural belief about being homeless, must be considered as significant interrelations having an impact on the developing person. All of these interrelations are either supportive or destructive, and for the homeless child, it is becoming increasingly more supportive.

In the background information discussed by Bassuk (1987) on the families studied in the Boston area, influences on development were stated as a possible cause to homelessness:

> Various economic factors have contributed to the recent emergence of homelessness among families. These include the breakdown in family structure in association with poverty, the housing crisis, and reduced welfare benefits. Based on our preliminary data, I will argue that it is not only the economics of

> poverty that has created the new phenomenon of homeless families, but the combined efforts of poverty, violence, and profound deprivation on a person's development and self-esteem (p. 20).

A person experiences an event or happening, within a setting or context, consequently, a personal experience is never detached from the setting in which it occurs. The environment shapes the cognitive, social, and emotional aspects of the developing person; therefore, the personality and total life are influenced by the surroundings as well as significant individuals within the surroundings. Within that environment, stimulus deprivation and over stimulation, especially with an inability to control the situation physically or psychologically, become detrimental to the developing person (Rivlin, 1990).

In further analysis of the ecological environment of the homeless child, Rivlin (1990) depicted the power of "personal place."

> For children, establishing proprietary interests over places at home is one means of obtaining a sense of security, away of mastering the stimulation, expectations, and other social and intellectual demands of the outside world. At the same time, it contributes to the identity of the child . . . Without romanticizing their functions, roots or attachments serve to define the world and prevent alienation . . . A close and careful consideration of all kinds of homeless persons is needed to understand the ecology of homelessness and to delineate its impacts on children (p. 13-15).

Bronfenbrenner (1986b) listed studies that suggest families moving from place to place can be a major predictor of the child's later development. Relocating for the homeless child can change shelter, school, peers, and family. If just one of these "worlds of childhood" is disrupted the child can experience "alienation" (Bronfenbrenner, 1986a, p. 430). If this disruption is prolonged, the results may have a powerful influence on the developing person. This also affects their education. "Children who feel rootless or caught in conflict at home find it difficult to pay attention in school. Once they begin to miss out on learning, they feel lost in the classroom" (Bronfenbrenner, 1986a, p. 431).

In discussing what schools can do to prevent alienation, Bronfenbrenner (1986a) suggested concentrating more on teaching productive citizenship: becoming a productive member of society, behaving well toward others, and learning responsibility to community and nation. The curriculum should include learning and engaging by caring which might include locating day care centers of children and the elderly adjacent to the schools. The schools need to attempt this restructuring, not only because they have the most to gain but also,

> . . . the school is the only place in which all children gather every day. It is also the only institution that has the right (and the responsibility) to turn to the community for help in an activity that represents the noblest kind of education: the building of character in the young (p. 436).

CHARACTERISTICS OF HOMELESS CHILDREN

Gonzalez (1990) made the point that "the psychosocial needs of the children (both transient and permanent) are as important as their instructional needs, because these children suffer the combined effects of poverty, anxiety, and depression" (p. 787). Hartman (1989) stated "the existence of homelessness provokes a variety of responses: anger, outrage, guilt, shame, and perhaps most devastating, an overwhelming sense of helplessness" (p. 483). Bassuk and Rubin (1987) listed "developmental delays and severe depression or anxiety and learning difficulties" as deficits found within homeless children (p. 279).

> Emotional and socialization problems are common consequences of homelessness. Many homeless students are under severe stress and act depressed or aggressive. Students are often embarrassed to tell anyone at school about their life-styles and therefore have a difficult time socializing with peers (Wells, 1990, p. 32).

The preschool age homeless children Bassuk (1987) interviewed revealed significant deficits in the social, emotional and cognitive areas, including "difficulty with language, sustained attention to task and physical coordination" (p. 22). Bassuk (1987) also stated that half of the homeless children evaluated for psychological difficulties required further psychiatric evaluation. According to Eddowes and Hranitz (1989), "homelessness is devastating to children, taking a toll on health and emotional well-being. Homeless children have no place to call their own and few personal belongings" (p. 198).

In Philadelphia, Fox and Roth (1989) found the effects of homelessness on children included "poor health, limited access to a source of continuing health care, developmental delays, emotional disturbance, and poor school performance" (p. 141). Several of the studies listed by Rosenman and Stein (1990) found symptoms of homeless children to be withdrawal, depression, and suicidal feelings. Bassuk and Gallagher (1990) described behaviors of regression, e.g. eating and sleeping difficulties and bed-wetting. Aggressive or withdrawn behaviors were noted, e.g. anger, crying for no reason. Provocative, hard to control, and mothering behaviors were also described, e.g. siblings fiercely supporting each other and trying to nurture and discipline their own mother. Fox, Barrnett, Davies and Bird (1990) investigated 50 homeless children ages 4 through 10 years for emotional disturbances and developmental delays. They found 32% had high levels of emotional and behavioral disturbance, 74% had moderate to severe emotional impairment, and the great majority were functioning far below the average cognitive level.

Tower and White (1989) gave detailed histories of several homeless children. They demonstrated the complex unpredictable behavior of the parents and the uncontrollable events transpiring in the environment that are manifested in the lives of these children. "Such feelings of confusion in a child are typical. Homeless children feel hopeless and out of control of their lives. It is not uncommon for children to exhibit physical manifestations of their confusion and worry" (p. 18).

DEPRESSION AND HELPLESSNESS IN HOMELESS CHILDREN

Children are considered helpless when they view their situation as uncontrollable. They have learned no matter what they say or do the environment does not change. As Seligman (1975) profiled the theory of helplessness, it becomes relatively easy to imagine a homeless child.

> This, then is our theory of helplessness: the expectation that an outcome is independent of responding (a) reduces the motivation to control the outcome; (b) interferes with learning that responding controls the outcome; and, if the outcome is traumatic, (c) produces fear for as long as the subject is uncertain of the uncontrollability of the outcome, and then produces depression (p. 55-56).

In a behavioral-cognitive theory of helplessness, Seligman (1975) depicted the uncontrollable situations in a person's life as causing three types of disruptions: "the motivation to respond is sapped; the ability to perceive success is undermined; and emotionality is heightened" (p. 44).

Although the homeless children are affected physically due to a lack of medical attention, physical illness can also be psychological as in the case described by Tower and White (1989).

> It is not uncommon for children like John to exhibit physical manifestations of their confusion and worry. John's vomiting appeared to be indicative of his concerns about home rather than an actual illness . . . As a result not only of their life-style but also of dietary limitations, children and youths can be listless and withdrawn. Depression is a common companion. For some children, depression and stress get translated into hyperactivity, an inability to stay within the structure of rules, and often aggressive, hostile behavior (p. 18-19).

These homeless children are further described as depressed, moody, and having a low tolerance for frustration (Gewirtzman & Fodor, 1987);

having "a precursor to learned helplessness" (Whitman, et al., 1990, p. 516); "an overwhelming sense of helplessness" (Hartman, 1989, p. 483); "a sense of hopelessness and a life out of control" (Balfour, 1991, p. 30); and "the loss of self-esteem . . . perceptions of failure and helplessness" (Eddowes & Hranitz, 1989, p. 198). Of the 212 homeless youth extensively interviewed in Amsterdam, Holland, Ploeg (1989) suggested

> over 50% have a fatalistic belief that their destinies are determined by factors outside themselves such as fate, luck, chance, powerful others, etc. We also found symptoms indicating that the youngsters investigated do not function adequately in physical, psychological, and social respects (p. 53).

Bassuk, Rubin and Lauriat (1986) investigated 151 homeless children in Boston ranging in age from 6 weeks to 18 years. The school-aged children were tested with the Children's Depression Inventory and the Children's Manifest Anxiety Scale which revealed approximately 50% required referral for psychiatric evaluation. This result was also indicated on the Schenbach parent checklist concerning two-thirds of the boys and one-half of the girls aged 6 to 11 years and one-third of the 13 children tested aged 12 to 16 years. Of the 52 children, 21 were failing or performing below average academically, 25% were in special classes, and 43% had already repeated one grade. Parents reported 12 children required constant medical care from a physician and one-fourth had emotional or development problems. These researchers further stated that studies investigating homeless children needed "systematic clinical data" of their developmental and emotional status (p. 1097). Bassuk (1987) later indicated that most of the homeless children verbalized suicidal thoughts and the overall depression scores were as severe as a comparable psychiatric population.

Fox, et al. (1990) evaluated 50 homeless children in the New York City area. Parents completed the Achenbach Child Behavior Checklist (CBCL). A child psychiatrist interviewed each child and gave them a score on the Children's Global Assessment Scale (CGAS) which assessed the lowest level of functioning in the past month and at six month intervals. They were assessed with the Peabody Picture Vocabulary Test (PPVT) and the Developmental Test of Visual-Motor Integration (VMI). Cognitively, 40% scored below the 10th percentile on the VMI and 61% were at the 1st percentile on the PPVT. Emotionally, 32% presented with high levels of emotional and behavioral disturbance according to the CBCL and on the CGAS 74% indicated moderate to severe impairment.

Whitman, et al. (1990) evaluated 139 children ages 5 months to 18 years in a shelter in St. Louis, Missouri with the Slosson Intelligence Test-Revised (SIT) and Peabody Picture Vocabulary Test-Revised (PPVT-R) for cognitive assessment. The House-Tree-Person drawing test was used for emotional assessment. The results suggested approximately 35% of the SIT scores, 63% for boys, and 71% for girls on the PPVT-R were in the mentally retarded or borderline range. Emotionally, "few children displayed significant emotional pathology in their drawings, and none of the drawings qualified as extremely bizarre or deviant" (p. 517).

Gewirtzman and Fodor (1987) suggested a way to help homeless children who may have difficulty verbalizing is to have them draw. This would allow the researcher an opportunity to view their feelings through symbolism. Horowitz, et al. (1988) evaluated the importance of school setting by administering the Student Survey Questionnaire to 38 homeless children, 48 poor children with homes, and 42 community children. The results suggested 80% of the homeless children reported they wanted to attend school compared to 62% of the poor and 62% of the community children, which may suggest that the homeless children do indeed see the school as a positive aspect within their somewhat chaotic world.

SUMMARY

While homelessness is a problem centuries old, the rise in homelessness is a very recent and puzzling problem to an affluent society. Within the ecology of homelessness exists one aspect of the problem, that of educating the homeless children, which not only affects the lives of the homeless individuals of today but our nation and society of tomorrow.

The theoretical framework of this study consists of the ecology of the process of educating homeless children that encompasses a comprehensive and a fundamental level (Bronfenbrenner, 1979). The psychological aspects of the homeless children are considered within the Theory of Helplessness (Seligman, 1975). While the response of many states to the education of the homeless children has been accelerated through federal funding, research on the process of that response has lagged.

A review of the literature provided invaluable information to be used in the intervention and prevention of homelessness. Within the literature, the barriers to effectively educating the homeless children have been well documented. This study affords the opportunity of an intimate view of the interaction among the systems that propose to eradicate those barriers.

While there are many studies describing the personal characteristics of homeless children, information on how a transitional center attempts to respond to their needs is nonexistent.

III

Methodology

STATEMENT OF THE PROBLEM

The first purpose of this research was to analyze and describe the response of Morgan County* to educating homeless school-age children within the context of the ecology of homelessness. The second purpose of this study was to investigate the characteristics and perceptions of the homeless children. Both components of this study were explored in an effort to understand and thereby enhance the process of educating homeless children.

PHILOSOPHICAL AND METHODOLOGICAL RATIONALE

The authors hold to the philosophy that development is influenced by both the individual and the environment. Hamm (1981) stated the pragmatist "believes both the child and society are important . . . heredity and environment are persuasive in the making of man" (p. 40-41). The pragmatic philosophy meshes psychology and sociology. Both are important in understanding the organism in its environment or the student in the educational setting. This research attempts to understand the reality

---

*The names of all persons and places have been changed to provide anonymity.

of educating homeless children through describing both the environment and perceptions of the homeless children.

According to Bogdan and Biklen (1982), reality for the phenomenologist consists of the meaning of a person's experiences through interacting with others. Phenomenology is the study of that which is being experienced by the individual at any given moment. The phenomenologist utilizes unstructured interviews to probe the human experience and interpreting the experience to the informant validates understanding. Renata Tesch (1984) described three research questions explored by the phenomenologist:

> Basic inner processes experienced by everyone at some point in life; experiences believed to be important sociological or psychological phenomena of our time; and changes or transitions that are very common or of special importance . . . Phenomenological research is valuable to empathetic understanding. It may also be of great value to educators and other professionals involved with children (p. 1).

While the phenomenologist may believe that reality is totally subjective, the ethnographer recognizes the objective reality as well, which denotes an interaction between culture and the meanings people attribute to events. "What makes a study ethnographic is that it not only treats a social unit of any size as a whole but that the ethnography portrays events, at least in part, from the points of view of the actors involved in the events" (Erickson, 1984, p. 52).

Ethnography often utilizes several research techniques. In Wolcott's (1979) taped lecture and study guide, many ethnographic techniques are discussed. Participant observation allows the researcher to be both a participant and observe in the social setting. Interviewing may consist of several forms, i.e. interviewing a key informant or an informative individual, interviewing for a life history, interviewing with a structured formal or informal question sequence. Questionnaires or formal surveys are used when appropriate. Projective techniques such as the Thematic Apperception Tests may be incorporated into the research design and standardized tests may be used, although adjustment to administrative rules of some instruments may be necessary. Formal documents or other written sources less formal such as journals and letters may be accessed.

Non-written records including photographs and films may also be examined.

The ethnographic and phenomenolistic research techniques used in this study were guided by the research questions and population being studied. The data collection techniques of ethnography that were used in this study included participant observation, interviews, surveys, projectives, journals, and standardized tests such as self-report measures. The phenomenological techniques included interviews and journals.

RESEARCH OBJECTIVES

This study explored two levels of the program Hopeful Horizons. First, the ecology of the homeless children was explored by analyzing and describing the systems which may both enhance and impede education. Second, the phenomenological aspects of the homeless children were explored. The specific objectives providing the framework for this study are contained in Table 3-1.

DATA GATHERING TECHNIQUES

As one of the purposes of this study, the evolution of this program was investigated using a weekly journal, observations, interviews, and surveys documented by the researcher. Initial interviews explored the vision each individual on staff had of the program in the beginning and later interviews targeted how that idea may have changed. However, all interviews were loosely structured in direction allowing the informants to explore all aspects including their emotional involvement in the program. Interviews with the individuals who met at the program's conception and named the program Hopeful Horizons were conducted. The monthly meetings of the community board organized for the planning and continued support of Hopeful Horizons were attended to ascertain the mood of change represented in the meetings.

Table 3-1. Research Objectives.

Research Objective 1

To describe the evolution of Hopeful Horizons as a response to educating homeless children.

Mode of Inquiry

Ethnographic

Data Collection Technique

Interviews
Observations
Pre and Post Surveys

Research Objective 2

To describe the perceptions of motivation, success in school, the emotional indicators of anxiety, depression and helplessness, and family-life by the homeless children.

Mode of Inquiry

Ethnographic
Phenomenological

Data Collection Technique

Projectives
Journals
Self-Report Measures
Interviews
Time on Task

The following represents a summary of the time spent and instruments developed during the research and evaluation of this program.

1.Observations: 49 visits 377 hours

2.A total of 62 interviews of approximately 30 to 45 minutes each were conducted with students, parents, grandparents, staff and volunteers, community board members, district administrators, shelter administrators, and school principals and teachers.

3.Two survey instruments were developed and administered to staff and volunteers as pre and post measures of perceptions regarding program effectiveness, goal orientation, and recommendations for improvements.

4.Documents and records were examined:

(a)Program policies and procedures manuals;
(b)Student data records;
(c)Program brochures;
(d)Community Board meetings, minutes, and bylaws.

Another purpose of this study was to gain understanding of both the program and the homeless children within the program by utilizing several ethnographic and phenomenological techniques. In an attempt to understand the experience of homeless children, interviews and daily journals written by them were explored for their perspective. The interviews consisted of the researcher bringing to the interview only a brief knowledge of each child. They were then encouraged to share the phenomena of being homeless; however, the younger children had difficulty expressing themselves verbally. This was anticipated and the daily journals kept by the children with drawings in them helped detect the changes in the process of being educated as a homeless child.

The psychological assessment of the children consisted of several instruments and techniques. Projective techniques, standardized tests, and time on task were used in assessment. The magnitude of motivation to respond was observed during testing by recording the time spent on several tasks to determine if "the motivation to respond is sapped," as indicated in Seligman's theory of helplessness (1975, p. 44). The following instruments were administered to detect indications of anxiety, depression, and helplessness:

(a)The Bender Gestalt Visual-Motor Test, (1946);
(b)House-Tree-Person Drawings (Ogdon, 1986);
(c)The Reynolds Child Depression Scale, (1989);
(d)The Reynolds Adolescent Depression Scale, (1989);
(e)The Piers-Harris Self-Concept Anxiety Scale (1969).

The Piers-Harris Self-Concept Intellectual and School Status Scale (Piers & Harris, 1969) was administered to determine attitude toward school and intellect. The Kinetic Family Drawing (Burns, 1982) was administered to investigate the perception of family-life of the homeless students.

LIMITATIONS

The limitations of this study were due to the population studied, the setting, and assessment procedures. The homeless population was extremely mobile and this high degree of transiency precluded the customary pre-post assessments. To find these students at a later time in order to assess the long-term effectiveness of a program of this kind is close to impossible.

In the setting, a limiting factor was the ceiling number of 30 homeless children at any one time within the program due to lack of space and personnel. Having only one after school hour available restricted the depth of interviewing, especially with teachers, and other data gathering procedures. This may have had an effect on the findings. Most personnel were not available after hours or on the weekend.

The emerging concept of Hopeful Horizons stayed in constant flux requiring a flexible, shifting, adaptive methodology. Qualitative rather than quantitative methods were utilized considering the small numbers and transiency of the population, which prohibited the use of pre-post standardized assessments.

Being a participant-observer did not appear to influence the data except where the observations of the classroom were involved. The director and social worker seemed to adjust well to my presence, as evidenced by the statement made while driving on a field trip, "We probably shouldn't be talking this way but we forget and just think of you as one of us." However, at the first interview, a slight resistance from the teachers was detected. Efforts were made to correct this by eating lunch in their lounge, discussing students, vacations, etc., and spending more time in the classroom. As teachers left immediately after school, no after school hours for discussion were feasible.

The resistance became more evident when a volunteer expressed concern that she had been informed by the teachers that maintaining the journals was not priority as it had nothing to do with the evaluation. Nothing seemed successful in correcting this problem which may have influenced the data collected. This difficulty may be attributed to the dynamics of administrators evaluating employees and the teachers seeing my position as an evaluator, which may have been interpreted as threatening.

It was extremely difficult for the younger children to discuss their experiences of being homeless; they would rather explore the environment. The small number (n=5) of older students, ages 11-16, was limiting, but they gave significant information.

The parents were the most difficult to interview. They spent their days job hunting, house hunting, etc. and had very little time to spend with researchers. Usually they appeared to be in such crisis that they were relieved to have their children gone for the day at school. This gave them more free time to take care of the important needs of the family. These parents even found it difficult to come with the children the first day to enroll them and were seldom seen after that until the day they withdrew them from the program. The histories that were obtained on the 16 children in this study were either obtained from meeting the parents at the shelter or from a staff member who enrolled the child.

Limitations were often within the instruments chosen to measure the characteristics of the homeless children. The Bender Gestalt had an age limit of 12 years; however, another instrument that would provide comparable information, as to the measurement of time to complete the task, was not available. However, only one child reached the ceiling on this instrument.

The administration procedures of both the Piers-Harris Children's Self-Concept Scale and the Reynolds Child and Adolescent Depression Scales required adaptations for students unable to read well. The researcher read the statements to the homeless children and this may have influenced the results. These self-report measures may also bring an element of bias by the individuals desiring to project themselves as either more or less positively.

Another limitation may be found in the scoring of the House-Tree-Person Drawings and Kinetic Family Drawings. As with all projective measurements, there is an element of subjectivity of the researcher to be considered. This was minimized by simply counting the presence of indicators rather than interpreting the emotionality.

While the Bender provided an effective assessment of the motivation to respond in the nonverbal area, there was not an effective measure taken of the verbal motivation to respond. This may have influenced the findings, considering that some children have strengths in verbal ability and assessing the delay in that ability may have proved to be valuable information.

While the Kinetic Family Drawing as an assessment of family life is subjective, considering the limited vocabulary of the younger children, it was decided that this measure would yield the most accurate information.

The results of this study cannot be generalized to other educational programs for homeless children considering the unique evolution of this program. However, it may be conceivable that the information gathered and analyzed will be of some use to those contemplating similar programs. The successes and failures here may assist other professionals in predicting the outcome of their programs that are similarly structured. This report also may assist in the planning of future educational programming. The information regarding this program and personnel and the psychological characteristics of the homeless children presented are hoped to enhance the educational process.

IV

Results

In this chapter, the results of the research are reported. Included are descriptive data, complete tables of summary data, results of data analysis, and a explanation of the trends and patterns in the data.

This research examined the response of Morgan County to educating homeless children through the ecological aspects as well as the psychological aspects of the students. The first purpose was to investigate, through an ecological orientation, the systems that influence the evolution of an educational program designed to meet the needs of homeless children. The second purpose was to investigate, through a psychological orientation, the perceptions of the homeless children. Both views are an effort to explain the process of educating homeless children in a broad ecological and narrow individualized or psychological perspective.

The results will be presented in two separate but related units. The first deals with the district's attempt to provide education to the homeless children in their midst. The first section examines the three stages of the evolution of the transitional center. Stage one is a brief investigation of the origin of the program and explores the vision of the individual who conceived of Hopeful Horizons. Second, the district's composition of a proposal intended to acquire McKinney Funds is presented. Third, a perspective of reality is explored, looking at what really happened, the congruencies or incongruencies. The second section describes the children themselves regarding their psychological patterns of motivation, anxiety, depression, helplessness, and perspective of school success and family life. What has been learned by an examination of these students is presented in the second section and both sections will complete the information given in the results chapter.

THE VISION

Every story has a beginning; during a taped interview, Sarah described her desire to begin Hopeful Horizons. After reading a newspaper article about a school for homeless children and youth located in another state, Sarah Burns birthed a vision of doing the same in Morgan County. Her first step was to inquire at the Morgan County Public School District for funds which may be available. She describes her intent and their reaction during the interview:

> . . . I first went . . . to ask for help, encouragement, anything positive. I received nothing at all positive from them. Then I found the Salvation Army . . . would provide a couple of rooms. . . . I thought we were finally going to get . . . off the ground but . . . One of the administrators put too many obstacles in my path.

At this time Sarah had written a press release for a local newspaper that was picked up by a wire service and distributed all over the state. Then a local television station and radio station interviewed her and she describes the reactions:

> . . . I got many, many phone calls and many, many volunteers from all walks of life and age groups, and capabilities, because of the P.R. that I did, but the bureaucracy was growing and growing and . . . about to stop me completely.

Sarah had placed a phone call to another more prominent charity and received a $15,000 grant and a place to begin the school which would be located in a church. She began receiving textbooks, school supplies, library books, etc. from public schools all over the state. In May 1990, the Morgan County School District informed Sarah of possible federal funds that were being offered for an ongoing homeless education program. She was now included in all meetings to prepare the grant proposal but explained that she was not given primary consideration as the one who had conceived the program.

During the time these meetings were held, Sarah had several jobs and was recovering from a near fatal accident.

> . . . I knew my health would fail if I continued as director . . . after it opened up in the fall because the school (Morgan County District) would keep me enmeshed in their politics and bureaucracy and I knew I would have to fight for the real reason I had started . . . which was to help each little homeless individual that I could, not so much academically but in building his stability and self-esteem.

Sarah's husband had accepted a position in another state, and in June 1990, she communicated her vision to a friend, then convinced that friend to take the position at Hopeful Horizons, and moved to another state.

THE PLAN

Every vision must have a plan in order to succeed. The district provided leadership in presenting a proposal to the government that consisted of five major components: Educational, Social Service/Health, Counselor/Testing, Parent, and Volunteer.

According to the proposed plan (Biscoe, 1989, p. 10, 12, & 13) for Hopeful Horizons, there were to be five separate components to the program:

1. Educational Component
2. Social Services and Health Component
3. Counseling Component
4. Parent Component
5. Volunteer Component

Educational Component

First, full-time transitional teachers were to be hired to work at Hopeful Horizons. These teachers were to plan, diagnose, and provide individualized, supplementary educational programs to meet the individual needs of the homeless students as they were being processed for placement in the regular school setting. Volunteers were to provide assistance to the transitional teachers in the classroom setting. The transitional teachers were to assist the project director with training for the volunteer staff. A transitional team consisting of all key personnel at Hopeful Horizons was to develop a transitional plan for each student to facilitate placement in the regular school setting. The plan would specify current student status, as well as additional academic, social, and health needs. Students were to attend Hopeful Horizons from 8:30 a.m. to 3:00 p.m. during the regular school year. During the summer months Hopeful Horizons was to remain open for processing students and basic remediation and tutorial needs. If students were still residing within the school district's boundaries when school began in the fall, they were to be immediately assigned to a regular school setting.

Social Service/Health Component

A full-time social worker was to be hired to network with the shelters in identifying school-age children who should be attending school. The social worker was to work at Hopeful Horizons full-time and gather data to assess health, clothing, and other social welfare needs and work with volunteers to collect donations for needed items. He/she would make referrals for other services which might be needed by the family. In addition, the social worker was to accompany the children one day a week to the County Health Department for health check-ups and needed immunizations and make school visits to confer with school staff to assist students with their social adjustment and transition.

Counselor/Testing Component

A full-time counselor was to be hired to develop and plan a counseling program and form support groups for homeless children needing emotional assistance. The counselor was also to have testing skills and be responsible for administering assessments necessary to determine academic and skill levels of students upon entry into the program. In addition a .50 FTE speech language pathologist was to be hired to identify and evaluate any speech language problems which might be interfering with the child's ability to learn. The pathologist would administer appropriate developmental assessments to determine developmental lags. The function of this position was to inform receiving schools regarding factors which might interfere with learning.

Parent Component

A goal of the program was to encourage parent involvement in all aspects of the child's education and to assist parents with workshops which would help them learn to access social and educational systems. The Community Center had agreed to work with parents by providing training for them through their Vocational Program for the Homeless. In addition, the center was to be of assistance in providing parents with outpatient therapy or crisis intervention services if needed.

Volunteer Component

Forty volunteers were recruited for Hopeful Horizons. The project director and transitional teachers were to have primary responsibility for developing a training program for the volunteers. Volunteers were to work in a variety of capacities, i.e. tutors, teaching assistants, resource developers, etc. The project director was to develop a training manual for use with volunteers which could be replicated and used in other programs. The project goal and seven objectives to assist with meeting that goal were then stated in the proposal (Biscoe, 1989).

Project Goal

To provide comprehensive educational and social services to 60% of the homeless children identified during the course of the year.

Objectives

1.The first objective was to develop an educational center that would provide comprehensive educational, social service support, and assessments to 800 homeless students during the course of the year.
2.The second objective was to identify and recruit 800 homeless students for placement in Morgan County District through its satellite Hopeful Horizons during the course of the year.
3.The third objective was to assess and place 60% of the homeless students identified in regular school settings.
4.The fourth objective was to provide a specialized 6.0 hour school day for students at Hopeful Horizons for a maximum of 2.5 weeks.
5.The fifth objective was to train the 40 recruited volunteers to provide tutoring, assistance, life skills development, and recreational alternatives and to develop resources for homeless youth.
6.The sixth objective was to follow-up on 15% of students placed to assess progress and adjustment to the regular school setting.
7.The seventh objective was to provide two hours of parent training for 100 parents during the course of the year.

THE REALITY

Having moved from the vision to a more concrete plan, the reality of that plan is now presented in the initial study of the 1990-1991 school year and the follow up study of the 1994-1995 school year. Every plan changes from vision to reality. What changes came about? Did the school fulfill the proposal in the first year or even in the fifth year of the program? Through observations and interviews, each component of the proposal was examined and will be discussed in the following section.

Components of the Plan

Educational Component

In the 1990-1991 school year, the Educational Component was fulfilled with the hiring of two teachers; however, the time required to plan, diagnose, and provide individualized educational programs (IEP) was difficult to find. Volunteers needed to assist these teachers on a daily basis were often not available; consequently, training volunteers became the sole responsibility of the Project Director assisted by an administrative secretary. The Transitional Team, consisting of the Director, two teachers, a social worker, and a speech and language pathologist, met once a week to assess student academic, social, and health needs and develop the transitional plans.

In the 1994-1995 school year, the staff included the Director, an administrative secretary, three teachers, two teaching assistants, a social worker, a family counselor, a social work assistant, and a psychologist as a consultant. The Transitional Team was able to meet daily when the children were sent home at 2:30 p.m. A tracking form was developed on every student which allowed any staff member to refer a student for assessment of academic, social, and health concerns.

Social Service/Health Component

The one social worker on the Transitional Team left the program in the spring of 1991. The program was experiencing financial difficulty, which severely restricted the funds designated for the social service personnel. An individual in the community heard of the funding problem and donated one year's salary for a social worker, who was hired in August of 1992 by the YWCA and continues in the program today. She had extensive prior experience working with both homeless children and domestic violence.

While it was difficult to fulfill the social component with one social worker, by the 1994-1995 school year the addition of a counselor and social work assistant allowed more time to network with the shelters and other community agencies, as well as transporting the students for physical examinations and immunizations. The social worker described the receiving schools as oppositional when making school visits to assist students with enrollment. That opposition has diminished somewhat but still persists even within the large school district of which Hopeful Horizons is a part.

Counselor/Testing Component

The full time counselor was nonexistent the first two years of the program. Those duties of providing support groups for the students and individual counseling as needed were given to the one social worker (1990-1991). The social worker held groups for one hour every day, which gave the teachers their planning period, but compelled her to work from 8:00 a.m. until 6:00 p.m. or even later, while the teachers' hours were 8:30 a.m. until 3:30 p.m., as employees of the public school. The position of the Speech and Language Pathologist was eliminated after the first year due to the referral process of the public school which prevented services from being provided in a timely manner and resulted in no services provided to the students.

The assessments of academic skills was screened by the teachers, and a consultant psychologist was retained by the community board to provide screenings of cognitive, developmental, behavioral, and emotional functioning of the students referred by the Transitional Team.

The salary of the social worker was provided by the McKinney Funds from the second year to the present. The counselor was hired by the YWCA in the third year of the program to give .50 FTE to the YWCA and .50 FTE to Hopeful Horizons. The social work assistant was added by the public school to the team in the 1994-1995 school year and has been able to assume many of the administrative duties of both the social worker and counselor, who have been able to maintain more reasonable working hours. The consultant psychologist has remained with the program, developing a Summary Score Sheet incorporating the tests given, making recommendations to the receiving school of the transitional students, and assisting with the training of the volunteers who acquired the duties of academic screenings of the students.

Parent Component

Parental involvement has been limited partially due to few personnel but also to the unavailability of the parents themselves, who are overwhelmed with locating housing and the process of obtaining government assistance to feed and clothe their families. In the 1990-1991 as well as the 1994-1995 school years, vocational training of parents has not been feasible both financially and practically. The social worker stated that initially she began working with parents in a rather directive manner which resulted in expending a significant amount of energy as she "pushed and pulled" them toward solutions. After realizing that the families were in such crisis and often unable to follow through with recommendations, the social worker then changed her "philosophy" and approach. Rather than providing information and networking with other agencies on issues she felt were important, in the initial contact with parents, they were asked, "What issues do you see as urgent and need assistance with?" Additional services to the battered womens shelter are offered by the counselor through the YWCA which constitute approximately 50% of the parents of the children at Hopeful Horizons.

Volunteer Component

With the first two years of the program, personnel were not available to properly recruit and train volunteers, resulting in five volunteers being involved with Hopeful Horizons on a weekly basis. However, the director that began in September of 1993 with Hopeful Horizons came with prior experience which included being the training coordinator for R.E.A.C.H., a network of casemanagers for the homeless. As a past President of the Junior League, she has been able to network well within the community to pull in volunteers on an as needed basis such as when taking the students on field trips and has involved at least 50 volunteers in the 1994-1995 school year.

Objectives 1990-1991 and 1994-1995

Concerning the objectives, objectives one and two were fully met with the exception of formal training for the staff, which was not provided in 1991 or 1995. The total number of students served by Hopeful Horizons from August 1990 through May 1991 was 108, and from August 1994 through May 1995, 293 homeless children were served. Although efforts continue to recruit through shelters, these students are difficult to identify, but all those identified were served. Objective three was met except for the limitation of the length of stay of a 2.5 week. In the first year, the average stay was 30 days and 21.2 days in the fifth year. With objective four, all the students that stayed in the district were eventually placed but the time it took to place them varied greatly. Objective five dealt with training volunteers. The first training session was not held until June of 1991; however, thereafter all volunteers initially received an orientation consisting of two to three hours of training and this continues to be an ongoing process. Objective six was met through follow-up by the social worker of the children placed in the district; however, no statistics were kept on the results. In the 1994-1995 school year, the Transitional Team incorporated a new strategy to ensure an 80 to 90% follow-up of all students leaving Hopeful Horizons. Part of the strategy includes a "Goodbye Backpack" filled with school supplies, a book with a special message from the child's teacher, and dental supplies and new socks, if needed. In addition to the backpacks, the teachers talk with each child about all the new opportunities possible in a larger school setting and encourage them to look for a special friend/advocate in the new school setting (excerpted from Hopeful Horizons Annual Report, 1995).

The special message from the teacher is written as an encouraging letter to the students, to which the students have responded well after moving to their new location, by writing a letter to the class. Joanna wrote a letter and drew a picture of herself.

> Dear Mrs. Smith,
>
> Remember me I am Joanna Davis the girl from the Salvation Army Shelter. I don't live there any more, we've moved in to a beautiful apartment it has autoumatic dishwasher, electric stove, shower, and refregorator. It's a great apartment, when we first moved in I had my own room, but the bed was weak and John my brother, continued to jump on it and it broke. NOW I'm sharing a room with my sister. I have no problems with that just I'd like to have my own room, my own privacy, my own phone. Dec. 19, is my birthday. I'm not begging but if you're planning to get me something I hope it's a Barbie doll car. Well I gotta go.
>
> Sincerely,
> Joanna Smith
> P.S. Just wanted to let you know I'm doing O.K.

Parents may write a letter for the student who wants to respond to the teacher's letter but has poor writing skills or may be too young to write.

> Dear Mrs. Smith,
>
> First of all, let me say thank-you to you for your time and attention given to my son. His work with the computer is very impressive! . . . Also it makes a parent proud to have their child happy at school, especially during this crisis time in our family's lives.
>
> Thanks For Caring
> Carol

While objective seven was not completed, there was a program being developed at the end of the 1991 school year to train parents in parenting skills and make referrals for vocational training. Although limited resources have continued to impede the offering of parenting skills training, referrals for parenting, education, and vocational training are made daily. In 1994-1995, the Transitional Team also offered four (compared to the public school's two) parent conferences and provided transportation to interested parents resulting in 100% attendance.

After exploring the major components of the program, it would now be appropriate to view the program as it really functioned. A glimpse through the investigator's observation of a typical day may assist in understanding what the real Hopeful Horizons became.

A Typical Day at Hopeful Horizons

It was 8:00 a.m. and the office of Hopeful Horizons was congested with the sounds of school beginning. The teachers Mr. Green and Mrs. Bauer were arriving, pouring coffee, and checking in with the director Judy Collins for vital information before beginning the day. The students were brought in a van to the site from the shelters between 8:30 a.m. and 8:45 a.m. and breakfast was served as soon as they arrived. As the enrollment was constantly fluctuating, a count of 17 was taken immediately in order to plan for the day. A volunteer, Joe, drove the van from the shelters to the site and supervised the breakfast. The teachers appeared to be making a mental assessment as to the mood of the students as they arrived. Some were smiling and genuinely glad to be at school, some looked angry and didn't want to be touched or spoken to, and some were tearful having had "a fight before coming to school."

The students who had attended the day before were given duties for this day and those assigned to clean the tables and wipe up the floor began their tasks. Teacher called roll and 14 were present and three new students just walked in the door. They all stood for Pledge of Allegiance and were seated just as a student yelled out "journals" (these were the daily journals kept for the evaluation and research). Mrs. Bauer then handed out the journals and the students began writing or drawing pictures. Mr. Green took the three new students to one end of the open classroom and began the paperwork. A volunteer, Sam, took the two kindergarten students and began working with them. Mrs. Bauer then took the rest of the class and began the subject of the Land Run of 1889. After the story of the Land Run was read to the class, they each received a packet of pictures of the flag, flower, state seal, etc. They were then told to open the encyclopedia to the information on their state and color the pictures according to the examples. The older students, 11 to 16 years, assisted the younger students, 6 to 10 years, with coloring, cutting, and pasting. These students continued working on these projects until morning recess.

In the meantime, Mr. Green was dividing his time between orientation of the three new students and reading with two first graders. Sam continued working with the two kindergarten boys trying to teach them to write the letters of the alphabet while they were hitting each other and kicking each other under the table.

During recess, almost all of the students played kickball and tag. Two female teenagers, Donita and Cindy, walked to the office and sat explaining to Judy Collins, the director, that they felt too sick to go outside. Upon probing deeper by Judy, it was discovered that Cindy had been slapped by her mother the night before and told that she'd be put in a foster home if she didn't straighten up. Donita was trying to comfort Cindy by telling her similar stories of her own family life situation.

After recess they lined up to go to the rest room and minutes later screaming was heard from the boys' bathroom. The teachers scrambled to the rescue and discovered that one of the older boys, Tom, had turned the light out on the last young boy to leave the restroom, Rick (6 years old). Mrs. Bauer explained that all the boys knew that Rick would scream very loudly every time they turned the light out and thought it was funny. What they didn't know was that Rick had been sexually abused many times, usually at night, and even brief darkness was extremely frightening for him. An investigation began to find out who was responsible for turning out the light.

Then it was time for the student store to open which it did each Friday after morning recess. All the tokens that the students had earned for good behavior throughout the week were turned in to purchase toys, accessories, and candy. They were then given a firm reminder that anything purchased in the store must remain untouched until time to go back to the shelter or it would be taken away.

Students were back in the classroom and coloring on the pictures of the Land Run of 1889 resumed. Break for lunch was at 12:00 noon. The kindergarten students went back to the shelters after lunch. Another volunteer came in and supervised lunch so the teachers could eat in the lounge. At 12:55 p.m. school resumed and students were continuing to talk loudly. Mrs. Bauer gave a resounding reminder that those talking would be escorted to the principal's office. The younger students were seated in the media area and allowed to select a book and read. Matt had enthusiastically taken out 20 books, reading none of them, and Brian was throwing the books up in the air and trying to catch them. As the older students worked on the pictures, the new students were taken aside and given a math test used for placement at the correct math level. At 1:55 p.m. all pictures were collected and another volunteer entered the room presenting a project in art and assisted them in putting it together. She had selected hand kites, which were small kites manipulated by extending the arm and waving the kite through the wind. The students were allowed to choose the colors of paper and decorations for their kite. At 3:00 p.m. school was out and the students were placed on a van to go back to the shelters.

Mrs. Bauer took the opportunity without students present to discuss how difficult it was to assign homework. She stated that the most gifted student that attends the school, Donita, a female 11 years of age, could not even get her homework done. When asked why it was so difficult, the student replied, "If you lived in the kind of environment I do, you wouldn't have your homework either. You just don't know what it's like." Mrs. Bauer then stated concern that she might need to visit a shelter to observe the environment because Donita was right, she really did not know what it was like.

The Emerging Concept of Hopeful Horizons

Through data analysis of the first year of Hopeful Horizons (1990-1991), it soon became evident that the emerging concept of Hopeful Horizons meant different things to different individuals. In interviewing key informants of the district, community board, and Hopeful Horizons' staff, five major points of contention became evident and influenced the final reality of Hopeful Horizons. The beginning date, purpose, definition of homelessness, commitment, and responsibility were each points of contention and needed to be ironed out before some stability occurred.

One of the very initial tensions at the surface appears trivial; however, it was shown to have influenced the attitude of acceptance or lack of acceptance as expressed by the director. The date the school was recognized as beginning to operate became the first stress point in the triangular relationship of district, Hopeful Horizons staff, and community agencies.

Table 4-1. Differences and Similarities of Conceptualizations and Categorizations of Events.

	District	Hopeful Horizons Staff	Community Agencies
Beginning Date	11-90	8-90	2-90
Purpose	Transitional Center/Site	School	School
Homelessness Defined	Children and Youth with Families	All Homeless Children and Youth	All Homeless Children and Youth
Commitment	A Time Line End of Grant	A Time Line As Long As Job Remains	A Time Line Continuous (Incorporated)
Responsibility	District Policy	$$	$$

Beginning Date

In the initial interviews, the beginning of Hopeful Horizons was reported as three different dates. Later interviews revealed that the district had reported that 11-6-90 was the official date of opening as the grant money was appropriated to the state on that day. The director had actually begun school in August of 1990 after visiting many shelters and giving out information about Hopeful Horizons. She had 15 students in the back of a church which contained an entry way (used as a media center), a kitchen, an adjoining dining area with four rooms extending from the kitchen used as a library, an office, and two classrooms. When the district became involved, they closed it down from 9-22-90 through 11-6-90 as the building had not met safety codes. Repairs were made and they reopened 11-6-90 and later moved the facility to the first floor of one of the community agency buildings.

While this date may seem trivial, the director felt all of her hours of labor in personally visiting the shelters, tutoring in some of the shelters, and recruiting were unreported because it all took place before the beginning date the district reported. The district, on the other hand, could not acknowledge a school in operation before the building codes were in compliance. The community agencies specifically reported nine months of operation before the district even became involved. While verbally each faction reported different dates, eventually they all agreed, when alluding to Hopeful Horizons in any written form, that the starting date was in fact as the district had recognized it, November 6, 1990.

School or Transitional Center: A Blurred Purpose

The second point of tension, that initially seemed to be in the name, at a deeper level had influence on the actual purpose of Hopeful Horizons. During interviewing, the community agencies had reported the school having a name and receiving donations in February of 1990. It appeared one individual working on a Ph.D. had gained support and been given a $15,000 grant from a church through a charitable community agency to begin the "school" Hopeful Horizons. The same community agency that had supported the program from the beginning now became the leader in igniting other agencies to become involved and also paid one-half of the director's salary to support what they called a "school" for homeless children.

The interview notes further suggested the concept of "school" had begun to change to "transitional center or site." Originally both the community agencies and the director of Hopeful Horizons had indicated the concept "school" meant a separate school for homeless children to share their common experiences without embarrassment or barriers preventing their education. However, the proposal written by district personnel stated Hopeful Horizons would be a transitional site where homeless children would be given a period of transition to adjust before entering the larger school system.

Although the district, community board, and staff may have begun with separate concepts of "school," by the time Hopeful Horizons had moved location, there appeared to be unity in considering it as a "transitional site." This evidence appeared in the board meeting notes, on the letterhead of Hopeful Horizons, and in daily conversations.

The evidence is clearly presented during interviews with the director, Judy Collins.

> In June of 1990, I was hired by the community agencies for the half time position as principal of Hopeful Horizons . . . I was then interviewed extensively by the administrators of Morgan County District and officially hired October 1990 for the half time position as director.

The community agencies depicted Hopeful Horizons as a school with a principal but the district called it a center or site with a director. Until the funding was received November 6, 1990, a taut situation existed between the district and community agencies. The community agencies approved the building located at the small church but the district did not. Therefore, Judy spent the morning as a community agency employee at the school and afternoons as a district employee training and attending meetings with a district administrator.

Judy describes her reaction to being hired half time by the district and half time by the community agencies.

> I had always wanted to start a school from scratch . . . someone had to open a school, write a curriculum and hire personnel. Then we were shut down for repairs and reopened in November 1990 . . . the community agencies saw me as a principal but the district saw

> Hopeful Horizons as a transitional site not a school, therefore I was not a principal but a director.

Then in June 1991 Judy writes

> My recommendation for the most effective educational program to serve children/youth of homeless families would mandate the transitional nature of such a program. Segregating homeless students will not encourage survival as a contributing member of society.

Also on the printed material from Hopeful Horizons evidence of a change in thinking occurred. In February 1991, printed material contained the logo of a school house with a name and address. In May 1991, there appeared the name Hopeful Horizons and under that the words Transitional Education Center for Homeless and Displaced Youth.

What began as a concept of "school" where homeless children would come and stay for as long as necessary ended May 1991 becoming a transitional site or center where the children were moved into a school setting within two weeks.

Definition of Homelessness or Who Shall Be Served?

The question of homelessness being defined had not entered the picture until the social worker was hired in January, 1991, paid by the grant but hired and supervised by the community agencies. This became the third point of contention. During interviews, the social worker shared her concern over the differing definitions of homeless children. Recruitment began in full force in January, and soon it was discovered that the social worker and community agencies were defining homeless children differently than the district.

1.The social worker and community agencies were defining homeless children as including all homeless children and homeless youth, e.g. emancipated youth walking the streets or living in shelters.

2.The district was defining homeless children as those with their families living in the shelters. It was felt by the district that "street kids" would not mix well with homeless children in families. The director also expressed concern that they did not have the personnel to deal with youth who may be using drugs or carrying weapons. After some weeks of debate, only homeless children from families living in the shelters were recruited.

Obligations and Commitment

Analysis of the field notes revealed two key concepts which were consistently being discussed by all three concerned entities: the district, the staff, and the community agencies. The first concept was that of "commitment," which was the fourth point of contention. The district held fast that their commitment ended with the end of the grant. The staff suggested their commitment continued as long as their position was not discontinued for lack of funds. The community agencies declared a continuous commitment during interviews and incorporated their board with official Articles of Incorporation and Bylaws presented in the minutes of the April 5, 1991 meeting. While the definitions of "commitment" appeared to be a time line, the ending of that time of commitment seemed to be different for each one.

At the time the field notes were complete (August 1991), the district still held their original position; no grant--no commitment. The district had come to the conclusion that Hopeful Horizons was a very expensive program. If the grant ended, a suggestion had been made that the school would be moved to the back of a nearby elementary school and contained in one classroom. It seemed as though the district felt the program was a very small part of their entire system. The community agencies saw it differently. They claimed ownership and felt the "school" was a community effort of which the district was a part. It was considered a charitable program set up as other programs were which offered services involving donations and volunteers and a great deal of community involvement. They presented it to the media as a community program called Hopeful Horizons not as a Morgan County District School. They had begun without district involvement and pledged they would someway, somehow continue the "school." The staff also held the same position as the agencies and hoped they would be allowed to continue their work at Hopeful Horizons. Although most of the staff had offers to work for higher salaries, their commitment to homeless children was strong. They repeatedly voiced the importance and necessity of a program for homeless children. At the end of the school year, each one of them had restated a desire to continue working at Hopeful Horizons. They expressed a great deal of personal fulfillment that seemed more rewarding than an increase in salary.

Responsibility

The other key concept that was consistently discussed was one of "responsibility," which was the fifth point of contention recorded in field notes. However, this concept was defined differently. Both the community board and staff of Hopeful Horizons discussed responsibility in terms of financial support and both expressed the observation that district funds had not been appropriated to the program. The community board continuously sought funds for the program and at times gave of their own personal resources. A staff member of Hopeful Horizons had reported that it was not at all unusual to receive cash donations or personal checks from the board members immediately following a board meeting where the needs of the homeless children were discussed. The district discussed responsibility in terms of policy. If policy stated it, then they were responsible for it; if not, they were not.

At the close of the investigation, this contention also remained. The district continued to discuss policy and did not put any funds other than the federal monies of the McKinney Funds into the program. The community board was actively seeking funds within the community through radio and television announcements. It caused a detente (term frequently used by the center director) situation between the district and the community agencies that continued even after the refunding of $50,000 for the 1991-1992 school year was announced. The staff members repeatedly made comments of their concern that the district was not "taking responsibility" for the program. They expressed admiration of the community board giving money to the program and spending time with the children but were very concerned that the board may not find the funds to keep the program without district support.

The Maturing of Hopeful Horizons

While the emerging concept of Hopeful Horizons has been somewhat solidified, in the 1994-1995 data, of the five major points of contention, there remains some evidence of continued struggle. However, even the few areas of disagreement are not as fervently debated as they once were.

With the turnover of staff including the director at Hopeful Horizons, the beginning dates appear to have become consistent with the district's reported involvement of 11-6-90. In the present documentation of the "beginning of" Hopeful Horizons, the phrase "in the fall of 1990" is often quoted, which would be consistent with both the district's and Hopeful Horizons's report but not with the community agency board. However, each faction now reports in their written documents, "the fall of 1990," as the beginning of Hopeful Horizons.

The agreed upon shift from "school" to "transitional center" has since proven to have originated from the shift of philosophy of the United States Department of Education (USED). The USED originally had funded tutorial assistance for homeless children and youth through the McKinney Funds with the emphasis changing to those programs which had continued with the transitional approach. The interest was now in moving those students into the public school district as soon as possible. Hopeful Horizons has made this shift easily, thereby retaining the McKinney Funding.

The subtle difference of "school" versus "transitional center" continues to exist. The networking agencies and the general public lack understanding of "transitional center." The social worker provided insight. "We use 'school' and 'transitional center' interchangeably. It depends with whom I'm speaking to, especially if out of state, most people understand 'school' better." The community agency board members continued to use the term "school" during interviews with implications that the public tend to readily support a "school for the homeless." Therefore, in public speaking on behalf of funding for Hopeful Horizons, board members as well as staff members use the term "school" rather than "transitional center."

Another now subtle point of contention, which is not directly discussed, is the definition of homelessness; who will be served. Each potential student enrollment is reviewed individually. With the emancipated youth and those bouncing back and forth between living at home or on the streets, there appears to be too many legal restrictions to include this population at Hopeful Horizons. However, the staff suggested that they have "more independence" from district policy. "It's our call now." It was reported that while the initial director sought more guidance from the district, the Transitional Team currently makes those decisions. They now feel competent to decide the rejection or acceptance of a student for enrollment into Hopeful Horizons. Because of concerns, e.g. gangs, the staff and board members agreed to exclude all homeless youth that would change the dynamics of the center in a potentially negative direction.

The concepts of commitment and responsibility were again significant issues revealed in the 1994-1995 field notes. Hopeful Horizons appears to have become more integrated into the district which has in turn increased the district's commitment. In 1990-1991, the district voiced their commitment to Hopeful Horizons as ending when the McKinney Grant for that year ended. The district currently has listed Hopeful Horizons with their other alternative education facilities and invited the teachers to attend the Alternative Education Faculty meetings. The original staff members were unavailable for interview; therefore, one can only speculate as to why they are no longer with the program. The stress of working under the microscope with evaluations conducted by an outside agency, the constant reminder by the district and the director about the temporal positions they held, and the district's as well as community agencies' daily observations may have proved to be too much stress, or they may have been drawn away to other opportunities. The new staff members who accepted positions as early as 1992 indicated that the stability they felt about their positions may have been due to the community board members making public statements that Hopeful Horizons was now firmly established. As one staff member reported, "because the board members stated that 'we are here to stay,' we talk about our job as though it will always be here." The community board has repeatedly demonstrated their commitment with their proclaimed ownership of Hopeful Horizons. Approximately a third of the original board members have continued with their membership. One of those originally involved with Hopeful Horizons is presently the president of the board, Gail Patton. In looking back and reviewing the growth of Hopeful Horizons, she commented,

> Homelessness is a community problem not a school problem. The school district didn't support it (Hopeful Horizons) and this probably helped us to become independent. They didn't want the ownership, we did!

Two other original board members described the composition of the board changing from "hands on" people in the community, which were defined as "those who wanted to be involved in the community at the hands on level" to the "professional yuppy group," defined as those younger members who are not directly involved but feel a strong commitment. "If they say they'll do, they do it." The younger "professional members" of the board were apparently "finding a social connection" within the community and gained support for Hopeful Horizons.

One of the people, reported by staff and board members as accountable for the transformation in structure as well as philosophy of the community board, is an initial board member and current president of the board, Gail Patton.

She reorganized the board and formed various committees who then reported to the board. One committee was formed by contracting with two outside individuals, an attorney and business person, who were "younger" and agreed to volunteer to collaborate as a nominating committee. They then went out into the community, networking with other "younger" individuals who represented organizations all over the city and who desired to volunteer time to Hopeful Horizons. Consequently, those names the nominating committee submitted to the board as possible board members were "reflections of themselves."

In October 1994, she began the "Strategic Planning Retreats." The first retreat began by reviewing the vision of Hopeful Horizons, the obstacles blocking the vision, the strategies to overcome the obstacles, and the formulation of the "One Year Implementation Plan and Calendar."

The philosophy of the board changed under her presidency. As explained, "we don't micromanage." Delegation of duties appeared not only to be encouraged but expected. The autonomy of the director was suggested as part of the philosophy and possible explanation for the director's effectiveness. "We let her do her job."

The majority of staff members and board members, of those interviewed individually, collectively stated that the simultaneous transformation of the board and the employment of the second and present director of Hopeful Horizons explains in large part the success of Hopeful Horizons. The passing of the reins of the board from a "hands on" approach was coupled with the passing of a director who had been a career educator. She was pursuing a doctorate, had been a vice principal in the public school system, and saw her role as one of working closely with the public school district to create a permanent place for Hopeful Horizons within the system. In contrast, the present director of Hopeful Horizons came from a background in business, counseling, teaching in private schools, and volunteer work which included past president of Junior League. She saw her "mission" as one of creating and maintaining a role for homeless children and youth within the community. The word "mission" is extracted from an interview with two board members who stated that they had been impressed when initially interviewing the director and she had stated she felt "a calling" to be the director of Hopeful Horizons. That is when the board "felt sure she was the person for the position."

This entire program and all those involved have indicated an almost religious fervor of establishing and maintaining this program in order to serve the homeless children. When it is considered that Hopeful Horizons began in a building at a church and now has plans to move back into a building owned by a church, one is reminded that in the beginning of this country, schools were often held in churches with the communities very involved in the welfare of all children and youth. This same spiritual flavor permeates every thread that has been woven into the fabric of Hopeful Horizons. This theme of religious fervor being translated into innovative school practice has been well documented by Smith, Kleine, Prunty, and Dwyer (1986).

The current president of the community board and current director of Hopeful Horizons worked closely together to create a structural reinforcement of the older, less stable beginnings of Hopeful Horizons. Both the "Strategic Planning Retreat" and "Partnerships" provided the support columns of the restructuring period, which led to changes in the financial responsibility of the program.

The financial responsibility for Hopeful Horizons has drastically changed for the district. In the first year, there were absolutely no funds other than the designated McKinney Funds appropriated to Hopeful Horizons from the district. In their 1994-1995 annual report, Hopeful Horizons reported the district's contributions for the school year to be $90,000. The staffs' main contribution continues to be personal monies contributed as well as personal sacrifices of accepting salaries less than those available in other positions. During interviews, the staff members continued to sing the praises of the community board who had raised in excess of $135,000 in grants (excluding McKinney Funds), community contributions, and partnerships.

The partnerships are defined within the policy of Hopeful Horizons.

> Partnerships such as Hopeful Horizons provide a model for future programs. As a true collaborative, government, educational systems, social service agencies, corporations, foundations, civic groups, and concerned citizens join together in a coordinated effort to resolve community issues. This provides an

exceptional opportunity to maximize all resources--both human and financial. All contributions and support--materials, services, or funding, public or private--are utilized more efficiently by working together for a common goal.

To truly understand what makes such collaboration possible, an appreciation of the sacrifice and commitment made by each participating organization is essential. Hopeful Horizons Partners share in today's challenging economic climate, this is not a gift given or received lightly. The Partners of Hopeful Horizons look past their own organizational needs to recognize and meet the needs of the children and families they serve.

SUMMARY

It is clear that the ideals of volunteers on a community board and the policies of a large urban school board do not mix easily. In the first year, each issue saw the staff drawn toward the idealism of the community board, but in each case the policies of the school board won out. However, as the community board became more determined in their commitment and took more responsibility for the maintenance of Hopeful Horizons, the school board began to make concessions. Hopeful Horizons gained the best of both worlds, recognized as part of the district and declared ownership by the community.

THE CHILDREN

After examining the struggles and efforts to build a transitional center, it is important to closely examine the reason for these efforts. Who are the children? What are they like? What are their needs, their hopes, their worries, their concerns? This section describes the investigation of their status in 1990-1991 and 1994-1995 in several ways: demographics, perceptions of being homeless, motivation, perceptions of success in school, anxiety, depression, and helplessness.

Demographics, 1990-1991 and 1994-1995

Of the 108 homeless children enrolled at Hopeful Horizons during the entire 1990-91 school year, 16 were assessed for self perceptions, and 43 of the 293 enrolled were assessed in the 1994-1995 school year. Only those children staying more than five days were included as it took that much time to complete interviewing and testing for each study. Sixteen children and youth representing 10 families in 1990-1991 and 43 children and youth representing 32 families in the 1994-1995 school year became the representative sample of the population of homeless children investigated. Demographic information describing both samples of children appears in Table 4-2.

Informal Assessment of 1990-1991 Homeless Children and Youth: Self Perceptions of Being Homeless

The second objective of describing the homeless children was investigated in 1990-1991 with daily journals during their stay at Hopeful Horizons to view the phenomenological experience of being homeless. An effort was made to continue the journals after leaving the program; however, the students were unable to comply. These entries represent a composite drawn from first day perceptions and last day perceptions. No attempt is made to suggest change or lack of change; only the mood of the child is sought.

Table 4-2. Demographic Characteristics of Homeless Children and Youth (1990-1991 n=16, Families Represented=10; 1994-1995 n=43, Families Represented=32).

	1990 - 1991		1994 - 1995	
	n	%	n	%
Gender				
Female	9	56	20	46.5
Male	7	44	23	53.5
Age				
5	1	6	5	12.0
6	3	19	9	21.0
7	4	25	9	21.0
8	1	6	3	7.0
9	1	6	3	7.0
10	1	6	4	9.5
11	2	13	1	2.0
12	1	6	3	7.0
13	0	0	1	2.0
14	0	0	4	9.5
15	0	0	1	2.0
16	2	13	0	0.0
Race				
American Indian	1	6	2	5
Black	8	50	20	46
Caucasian	5	31	19	44
Hispanic	2	13	2	5

First Day Journal Entries

"Today, I feel sort of half and half. Not exactly happy, but not quite sad or angry, either. Being that everything is so different. I have all these changes going on all at once, and it's a bit much. But I'm keeping my guard up, and just taking whatever comes next."

"Mom I love you dad."

"I'm glad because I get to see my dad tomorrow."

"I want to out."

"I'm hape today."

"Yesterday I was sick when I went everywhere so I couldn't go outside so I drank some hot chocklet and I made me a palet and I watched t.v."

"I love rain, I hope it rain."

"Well I'm really glad that my family is in a hous, and I'm so happy to be able to have my cat in the house with us and have more freedom. But I still thank God for places like the Salvation Army, The Anex and as well the Passage Ways."

"When I get home I will play basketball on my skates with my new friend. . . . The breakfast was not good at all. My parents are doing to get separated, mabey even a divorce. My moms old paster . . . will help us if my mom does what he says. My mom put my step-father in jail for pulling my brother up by the hair, kicking him half way across the room. My mom said that if 'I put him in jail I can't go back to him.' I called my friend . . . and talked for at least 30 min."

Last Day Journal Entries

"Still feeling the same as I usually do."

"Turtles, house, scarey, the." - a picture of a house.

"I feel like going home."

"I'm mad."

"I fill good today, I fill good today."

"Yesterday I was on the heat pump and my cusin stuck me with a dart and I got him back."

"I feel happy today."

"Today I don't fell like being around people today I just fell like being alone."

"Today I have been here for three weeks."

These children seem to be preoccupied with relationships and their feelings about individuals in their lives. Interviews with the children were attempted; however, many were too young to express verbally what they were feeling and spent the time discussing unrelated issues or investigating the surroundings of the room. In interviews with the older students, it became evident that these students did not confront life as children but as adults with adult worries, e.g. paying bills, buying groceries, trying to make relationships work within the family, etc. This may be part of the reason these children do not seem to fit in today's society. The homeless child seems to operate as an adult in a child's body. They feel different; they are different, different but seeking sameness or consistency even in the refuge of a school.

Informal Assessment of 1994-1995 Children and Youth

Daily journals were not kept in the 1994-1995 school year; however, the "Goodbye Backpack" elicited many letters that provided insight into the children and youth. The following letter was sent to the teacher from a 14 year old.

> Dear Mrs. Smith,
>
> Hi. How are you doing? Fine I hope. Have you heard from Nolan? I haven't heard anything from them. If you write him, tell him I said Hi, and that I love him, please. I write him and Micheal all the time but I don't think they ever see the letters. So how is school going? I'm doing ok, but Biology is hard. And I really don't have any goff-off classes. I have basic plus Home-Ec. And Phys. Science. Home-Ec. Is OK but I can't sew. Did you take home-Ec. In school? Jeremy just got a raise. Only a quarter. But every little bit helps. He is going to start working full time. We have our own place now. Its a two-bedroom trailor for only $175 a month. And we have got a lot of stuff for our house too. We got all of it used, but it is very nice. Like we got a matching couch, loveseat, and footstool for $25. And we bought

> a table for $50 and payed $7.50 each for our chairs. And his dad took us out and bought us towels, pots and pans, cleaner, silverware, and lots more. And him Mom bought us a bed, gave us a nick-nacks and a vaculm. And his grandpa gave us a lot of dishes and stuff for the house. And his Aunt bought us fish for our house. And we also got a recliner. So all in all we are doing very well. There are a lot of people trying to help us out. Well I guess I'll go. Keep in touch.
>
> Love always,
> Marsha

This letter and others like it reveal that the children continue to be preoccupied with adult issues. How many youths this age are able to even care how expensive the furniture is or know the amount of rent or mortgage on an apartment or home? Many teenagers today would be embarrassed to admit that other people gave them silverware and towels. Hopeful Horizons provides an environment where these children do not have to be ashamed about being homeless because all the children there are homeless.

Formal Assessment of 1990-1991 Children and Youth

Second, more formal assessment procedures were used in 1990-1991 to provide a portrait of the Hopeful Horizons children. Measures were taken to determine the existence of helplessness within the homeless children. Seligman (1975) describes three conditions that precede helplessness: motivation to respond is sapped, ability to perceive success is undermined, and heightened anxiety is followed by depression.

Motivation

In order to determine if response was sapped, the Bender Gestalt Visual-Motor Integration Test was given and timed. Koppitz (1975) indicated several studies reported The Bender Gestalt Visual-Motor Integration Test has an average time for completion of 6 minutes and 20 seconds. Seligman (1975) suggested that a helpless organism will be slower to respond and this was measured by comparing the average completion time on the Bender of the 16 subjects with that of the average time reported by Koppitz. The 16 homeless children had an average Bender completion time of 5 minutes and 6 seconds and 25% took more than 7 minutes and 20 seconds to complete the designs. On this measure of time, it is suggested that the magnitude of motivation to respond had not been sapped but was within the average range.

The Bender provided further information to be considered. Koppitz (1975) discussed a study that published a table of standard scores for the Bender with a mean of 100 and a standard deviation of 15. On the Bender, 56% of the homeless children scored at 85 or below, which suggests a delay in visual-motor integration.

The 12 emotional indicators on the Bender protocol suggest a possibility of emotional problems, if three or more are present (Koppitz, 1975). The emotional indicators of the homeless children suggested a lack of planning ability, poor organization, poor motor coordination, and emotional instability. The number of homeless students exhibiting these indicators on the Bender are reported in Table 4-3.

These measures tend to suggest that while the homeless children may generally have the motivation to respond, a number of them seem to be delayed in the development of visual-motor skills, a fact that may impede their success in school. The emotional indicators of poor planning or organization and poor motor coordination and/or emotional instability may also influence success in school.

Perception of Success

Self report of success in school was measured with the Piers-Harris Self-Concept Scale of Intellectual and School Status. A score at or above the 70th percentile suggests a positive self-concept in relation to school-related issues. Scores between the 31st and 69th percentiles suggest average self-concept, and scores at or below the 30th percentile suggest a negative self-concept in relation to school-related issues. The percentile groupings of the homeless children's scores are presented in Table 4-4.

This measure suggests that 94% of the homeless children have a moderate to high self-concept related to school success. It would appear that their ability to perceive success at school had not been undermined.

Table 4-3. Bender Gestalt Visual-Motor Integration Test.

Emotional Indicators	n	%
Confused Order	8	50
Wavy Line	11	69
Dashes for Circles	0	0
Increasing Size	4	25
Large Size	2	13
Small Size	4	25
Fine Line	0	0
Careless-Reinforced Line	1	6
Second Attempt	1	6
Expansion	0	0
Box Around Design	0	0
Elaboration or Addition to Design	1	6

Thirty-eight percent had three or more emotional indicators on the protocol.

Table 4-4. Piers-Harris Children's Self-Concept Scale of Intelligence and School Status (n=16).

Percentile	n	%
70 and Above	7	44
31-69	8	50
30 and Below	1	6

Anxiety

Indications of anxiety, depression, and helplessness in the homeless children were measured. The Piers-Harris Self-Concept Scale of Anxiety was used to measure anxiety. Scores at or above the 70th percentile suggest low anxiety, scores between the 31st and 69th percentile suggest moderate anxiety, and scores at or below the 30th percentile suggest high anxiety. The percentile groupings of the homeless children's anxiety scores are presented in Table 4-5.

This measure suggested that 94% of the homeless children are experiencing moderate to high anxiety. This may significantly interfere with their ability to comprehend in the school setting and would suggest school personnel may need to structure the day to move at a slower pace with a considerable amount of repetition in teaching, especially for new concepts. It would also suggest that counseling might be necessary to help them deal with the anxiety.

Table 4-5. Piers-Harris Children's Self-Concept Scale of Anxiety (n=16).

Percentile	n	%
70 and Above	1	6
31-69	7	44
30 and Below	8	50

Depression

The Reynolds Child and Adolescent Depression Scales were used to gain a standardized measure of depression. According to the manual, two measures are considered significant: total scores at 80 and above suggest severe depression and total scores at 74 and below suggest further evaluation aimed at diagnosing potentially significant psychopathology (Reynolds, 1989, p. 9). The percentile groupings of the homeless children's depression scores are presented in Table 4-6.

Table 4-6. Reynolds Child/Adolescent Depression Scale.

Children (n=13)		
Total Score	n	%
80 and Above	2	15
74 - 79	4	31
Adolescents (n=3)		
Total Score	n	%
80 and Above	0	0
74 - 79	1	33

Total scores are acquired by summing the scores for all items after using the scoring key.

This measure suggests that 13% of the homeless children were experiencing severe depression and 19% needed further evaluation to determine the severity of depression. A study in Reynolds' Manual (1989, p. 9) reported a rate of 5.2% for severe depression in a school-based sample of children. Seligman (1975) discusses heightened anxiety being followed by depression as the emotional component preceding helplessness.

Of the six critical items listed in the Reynolds' Manual (1989, p. 10), it is suggested that if a child or adolescent scores at a clinically relevant level on four or more, the case should be viewed as serious regardless of the total score. Two protocols were found to have at least four of the six critical items at a relevant level. One had been identified as severely depressed by the total score, but one of the children had not previously been identified. The percentile groupings of the homeless children's critical items on the depression score are presented in Table 4-7.

Table 4-7. Reynolds Children and Adolescent Depression Scale (n=16).

Critical Items	n	%
6. I feel like hiding from people.	3	19
9. I feel that no one cares about me.	5	31
12. I feel loved.	5	31
13. I feel like running away.	5	31
14. I feel like hurting myself.	2	13
20. I feel I am no good.	5	31

A clinically relevant level is determined by an item score of 3 or 4.

With this one protocol added, 8, or 50%, of the homeless children would then be considered as demonstrating depressive symptoms.

Helplessness

The House-Tree-Person Drawings were also utilized as a phenomenological measure of depression, helplessness, possible trauma, and suicidal tendencies. An indication of depressive tendencies appeared three or more times on 81% of the drawings by the homeless children. An indication of a possible trauma appeared on 38% of the protocols. An indication of helplessness appeared on 25% of the drawings, and an indication of suicidal tendencies appeared on 25% of the drawings by the homeless children.

When compared with the abused-clinical, nonabused-clinical, and normal groups of children (Blain, Bergner, Lewis, & Goldstein, 1981), the homeless children fit the profiles of both the abused-clinical and nonabused-clinical more closely than the profile of the normal children. The percentile groupings of the homeless children's indicators are presented and compared to an abused clinical, nonabused-clinical, and normal population in Table 4-8. The item numbers are matched with the item names in the ledger following Table 4-8.

There seemed to be a high degree of anxiety and depression demonstrated by the homeless children. While helplessness does not appear to be an overwhelming factor, the components said to precede helplessness are certainly present.

Table 4-8. House-Tree-Person Item Frequency of Compared Groups.

	Homeless		Abused Clinical		Nonabused Clinical		Normal	
	n	%	n	%	n	%	n	%
1.	2	(12)	8	(25)	4	(12)	0	(0)
2.	6	(37)	16	(50)	7	(22)	19	(22)
3.	4	(25)	5	(16)	4	(12)	3	(7)
4.	0	(0)	2	(6)	0	(0)	8	(18)
5.	7	(43)	20	(63)	19	(59)	9	(20)
6.	1	(6)	1	(3)	0	(0)	0	(0)
7.	0	(0)	0	(0)	0	(0)	0	(0)
8.	6	(37)	5	(16)	3	(9)	5	(11)
9.	2	(12)	11	(34)	7	(22)	4	(9)
10.	4	(25)	9	(28)	8	(25)	8	(18)
11.	4	(25)	4	(12)	5	(16)	10	(22)
12.	4	(25)	7	(22)	1	(3)	1	(2)
13.	2	(12)	4	(12)	2	(6)	3	(7)
14.	4	(25)	17	(53)	12	(38)	4	(9)
15.	6	(37)	16	(50)	12	(38)	8	(18)

Item Names:

1. Presence of person(s) (House)
2. Smoke present from chimney (House)
3. Door is above baseline with no steps leading to it (House)
4. Presence of clouds (House)
5. Absence of windows from ground floor (House)
6. House is transparent (House)

7. Ladders is leaning on trunk of tree (Tree)
8. Tree has fruit on its branches (Tree)
9. Size of limbs differ noticeably (Tree)
10. Eye is a circle with no pupil present (Person)
11. Paper is used as a base for a person (Person)
12. Figure is comprised of geometric figures (Person)
13. Multiple persons drawn (Person)
14. Absence of feet (Person)
15. Head is over 1/4 the total size of figure (Person)

Family Life

The perception of family-life of homeless children was measured with the Kinetic Family Drawing according to the manual published by Burns and Kaufman (1972). On the Kinetic Family Drawing, 63% of the homeless children depicted their families as helpless, without mobilization, and ineffective within the environment; 31% drew themselves closer in distance to the maternal figure; 38% depicted the maternal figure demonstrating nurturance and/or affection; and 69% depicted the family members without any interaction; each engaged in their own activity.

Formal Assessment of the 1994-1995 Homeless Children and Youth

The measures used for the subsequent years of Hopeful Horizons children and youth were chosen based on the needs of the children. The 1990-1991 assessment determined that the children appeared to have the motivation to respond, but many were delayed in the development of visual-motor skills. While most of the students seemed to have a positive self-concept in relation to success in school, they posed a serious challenge for the teachers who were attempting to provide successful academic experiences. To assist teachers in this process, students were screened for cognitive, academic, visual-motor integration, and emotional functioning. After leaving Hopeful Horizons, the Summary Score Sheet was sent along with other records to the receiving school. The social worker reported favorable feedback from the receiving schools in that the Summary Score Sheet provided academic assessment information that assisted in decisions concerning students who were possibly at risk for academic failure and may require an Individualized Educational Plan (IEP).

Of the 50 students we began with, 43 received complete screenings and provided the following data (seven were incomplete due to various reasons).

Cognitive Functioning

At the beginning of the 1994-1995 school year, the Test of Nonverbal Intelligence-2 (TONI-2) Form A together with the Peabody Picture Vocabulary Test-Revised (PPVT-R) Form M were used for cognitive screening. The Slosson Intelligence Test-Revised (SIT-R) was ordered but had not arrived. Therefore, eight of the students have two standard scores, the TONI-2 and PPVT-R, and the remaining 35 have one standard score, the SIT-R, as reported in Table 4-9.

Table 4-9. Cognitive Functioning Scores 1994-1995.

Category (Standard Score)		TONI-2	PPVT-R	SIT-R
Superior	120-above	0	0	1
High Average	110-119	1	0	3
Average	90-109	2	2	7
Below Average	80-89	3	1	6
Borderline	70-79	1	4	14
*Mild Mental Retardation	50-55 to 70	1	1	4
*Moderate Mental Retardation	35-40 to 50-55	0	0	0

*Diagnostic and Statistical Manual of Mental Disorders (DSM-IV).

Academic Functioning

The Wide Range Achievement Test-Revision 3 (WRAT-3) was used to screen academic functioning. Each academic subject of Reading, Spelling, and Arithmetic was then compared to the cognitive screening to determine if a significant discrepancy existed (two standard deviations below the cognitive standard score). Table 4-10 provides a summary of the standard scores of the academic screening.

Table 4-10. Academic Functioning 1994-1995.

Category (Standard Score)		Reading	Spelling	Arithmetic
Superior	120-above	2	0	0
High Average	110-119	2	3	0
Average	90-109	11	10	13
Below Average	80-89	10	10	12
Borderline	70-79	11	12	12
*Mild Mental Retardation	50-55 to 70	6	8	6
*Moderate Mental Retardation	35-40 to 50-55	0	0	0
Zero Raw Score		1	0	0

*Diagnostic and Statistical Manual of Mental Disorders (DSM-IV).

Visual-Motor Integration

The Bender Gestalt and Beery VMI Tests were used to screen visual-motor integration. The standard scores were compared to the cognitive functioning to determine if a significant discrepancy existed. Table 4-11 provides the summary of the standard scores of the visual-motor integration skills.

Table 4-11. Visual Motor Integration 1994-1995.

Category (Standard Scores)		Bender	Beery VMI
Superior	120-above	0	0
High Average	110-119	0	0
Average	90-109	1	12
Below Average	80-89	2	13
Borderline	70-79	1	6
*Mild Mental Retardation	50-55 to 70 (69)	2	5
*Moderate Mental Retardation	35-40 to 50-55 (49)	1	0

*Diagnostic and Statistical Manual of Mental Disorders (DSM-IV).

Emotional Functioning

Depression. The Reynolds Child and Adolescent Depression Scales were used to provide a standard score for depression and analysis of the critical items. The percentile groupings of the 1994-1995 homeless childrens' depression scores are reported in Table 4-12.

Two children were too low functioning to participate. The protocol was read to every child and youth with a low reading ability. One adolescent and seven children were identified as severely depressed and three children required further evaluation.

Table 4-12. Reynolds Child/Adolescent Depression Scale.

	1990	- 1991	1994	- 1995
Children	n=13		n=34	
Total Score	n	%	n	%
80 and Above	2	15	7	21
74-79	4	31	3	9
Adolescents	n=3		n=7	
Total Score	n	%	n	%
80 and Above	0	0	1	14
74-79	1	33	0	0

Total scores are acquired by summing the scores for all items after using the scoring key.

Of the six critical items listed in the Reynolds' Manual (1989, p.10), nine protocols were found to have at least four of the six at a relevant level.

Compared with the 50% of the 1990-1991 children and youth demonstrating significant depressive symptoms, the 1994-1995 screenings revealed 27% of the sample of children and youth with significant depressive symptoms, according to the Reynolds Depression Scale.

Table 4-13. Reynolds Children and Adolescent Depression Scale, Critical Items (1990-1991 n=16; 1994-1995 n=41).

	1990 - 1991		1994 - 1995	
Critical Items	n	%	n	%
6. I feel like hiding from people.	3	19	16	39
9. I feel that no one cares about me.	5	31	11	27
12. I feel loved.	5	31	9	22
13. I feel like running away.	5	31	10	24
14. I feel like hurting myself.	2	13	9	22
20. I feel I am no good.	5	31	9	22

A clinically relevant level is determined by an item score of 3 or 4.

Helplessness. In the 1994-1995 sample, the House-Tree-Person Drawings were also utilized as a phenomenological measure of depression, helplessness, possible trauma, and suicidal tendencies. An indication of depressive tendencies appeared three or more times on 79% of the drawings by the homeless children. An indication of possible trauma appeared on 33% and anxiety 56% of the protocols. An indication of helplessness appeared on 35% of the drawings and an indication of suicidal tendencies appeared on 21% of the drawings by the homeless children and youth.

When compared with the abused-clinical, nonabused-clinical, normal groups of children (Blain, Bergner, Lewis, & Goldstein, 1981), and the 1990-1991 sample of homeless children and youth, the 1994-1995 homeless children fit the profiles of both the abused-clinical and nonabused-clinical more closely than the profile of the normal children. The percentile groupings of the homeless children's indicators are presented and compared to an abused clinical, nonabused-clinical, normal population, and 1990-1991 and 1994-1995 samples of homeless children and youth in Table 4-14.

Family Life. The perception of family-life of homeless children was measured with the Kinetic Family Drawing according to the manual published by Burns and Kaufman (1972). In the 1994-1995 sample of homeless children and youth on the Kinetic Family Drawing, 79% of the homeless children depicted their families as helpless, without mobilization, and ineffective within the environment; 56% drew themselves closer in distance to a sibling than to either parent; 26% depicted the maternal figure demonstrating nurturance and/or affection; and 72% depicted the family members without any interaction; each engaged in their own activity.

Table 4-14. House-Tree-Person Item Frequency of Compared Groups (1990-1991 n=16; 1994-1995 n=43).

	1990-1991 Homeless		1994-1995 Homeless		Abused Clinical		Nonabused Clinical		Normal	
	n	%	n	%	n	%	n	%	n	%
1.	2	(12)	9	(21)	8	(25)	4	(12)	0	(0)
2.	6	(37)	7	(16)	16	(50)	7	(22)	19	(22)
3.	4	(25)	14	(33)	5	(16)	4	(12)	3	(7)
4.	0	(0)	3	(7)	2	(6)	0	(0)	8	(18)
5.	7	(43)	11	(26)	20	(63)	19	(59)	9	(20)
6.	1	(6)	5	(12)	1	(3)	0	(0)	0	(0)
7.	0	(0)	0	(0)	0	(0)	0	(0)	0	(0)
8.	6	(37)	10	(23)	5	(16)	3	(9)	5	(11)
9.	2	(12)	5	(12)	11	(34)	7	(22)	4	(9)
10.	4	(25)	8	(19)	9	(28)	8	(25)	8	(18)
11.	4	(25)	13	(30)	4	(12)	5	(16)	10	(22)
12.	4	(25)	15	(35)	7	(22)	1	(3)	1	(2)
13.	2	(12)	3	(7)	4	(12)	2	(6)	3	(7)
14.	4	(25)	13	(30)	17	(53)	12	(38)	4	(9)
15.	6	(37)	12	(28)	16	(50)	12	(38)	8	(18)

Item Names:

1. Presence of person(s) (House)
2. Smoke present from chimney (House)
3. Door is above baseline with no steps leading to it (House)
4. Presence of clouds (House)
5. Absence of windows from ground floor (House)
6. House is transparent (House)
7. Ladders is leaning on trunk of tree (Tree)

8. Tree has fruit on its branches (Tree)
9. Size of limbs differ noticeably (Tree)
10. Eye is a circle with no pupil present (Person)
11. Paper is used as a base for a person (Person)
12. Figure is comprised of geometric figures (Person)
13. Multiple persons drawn (Person)
14. Absence of feet (Person)
15. Head is over 1/4 the total size of figure (Person)

Summary of 1990-1991 and 1994-1995

All of these characteristics both in 1990-1991 and 1994-1995 may yield a typical profile of a homeless child when summarized, as the results and the analysis of the children and youth from the first to the fifth year did not change in profile. A typical profile would consist of a homeless child concerned about the relationships within the family. Motivation to respond to the environment would be within normal limits. A visual-motor delay may be present within this child which could suggest difficulty with school-related tasks. Poor planning, poor organization, poor motor coordination, and/or emotional instability may also influence success in school. The feelings about success in school would probably be either average or above which suggest a positive self concept related to school success exists. Anxiety would be experienced at a fairly high level and may interfere with the child's ability to learn in the school setting. There may be depressive tendencies but helplessness does not appear to be a dominant factor for the individual child. However, in viewing their own family, helplessness becomes the single most influential indicator. Therefore, it would seem that emotional instability is a factor that must be considered in any program educating homeless children.

V

Discussion

CONCLUSIONS

Vision Becomes Reality

When we left the intensive gathering stage in 1991 and looked ahead at Hopeful Horizons, the term Hopeful might have been a look into the future in doubt as to the achievement of its lofty vision. However, as demonstrated in the return visit of 1995 at a very different point in time, dream and vision appear to be very close to reality.

At one level, there are the readily visible daily changes and at another level there are two aspects which may be less visual but are probably more powerful: the influence of the director and the community board on the reality of Hopeful Horizons.

Hopeful Horizons grew in number of personnel from a director, a social worker, a .50 FTE speech and language pathologist, an administrative secretary, and two teachers in 1990-1991 to a director, a social worker, a counselor, a social work assistant, an administrative secretary, three teachers, two teaching assistants, and a psychologist as a consultant in 1994-1995. The number of volunteers increased from 5 to 50. The students served grew from 108 to 293. The Hopeful Horizons budget grew from the initial \$200,000 McKinney Funds plus a few small grants to \$355,768 of which only \$130,000 came from McKinney Funds. The building itself grew from three small rooms to a new location at the YWCA with three classrooms, a social work office, director's office, secretary-reception area, kitchen, a large conference room for group activities for the children, and a playground.

The concurrent replacement of the director of the program and the president of the community board after the first year seemed to have had a significant impact on the continuation of Hopeful Horizons. They both had extensive prior experience with volunteers and were successful at promoting projects within the community, partly due to their ability to network with other agencies and individuals in the community and partly due to the spiritual fervor to keep this program alive, which was intensely felt when interviewing either one of these leaders concerning the future of Hopeful Horizons.

Hopeful Horizons as an Ongoing Quest

Perceived success has kept the vision alive with new faces and new personnel. With the threat of losing their jobs diffused and the anxiety of depleted finances diminished, were they now becoming too comfortable? The social worker indicated a very real concern that the vision must be perpetuated. The continued success of Hopeful Horizons would require that they reinvest their capital of personnel into the original vision of Hopeful Horizons. The need for the vision then raised several questions which she had planned to explore by suggesting to the director a retreat for the personnel of Hopeful Horizons to provide an opportunity to "look back" at the original vision through discussion of responses to several questions.

1. Who are we as Hopeful Horizons staff?
2. For what do we stand?
3. What are we really doing here?
4. Where are we going?
5. How do we want to get there?
6. How can we better serve the homeless children and youth of Hopeful Horizons?

Regardless of further directions of Hopeful Horizons, the central problem being addressed should not be lost. That image of a homeless child is brought into sharp relief by the following narrative with which we close our book.

Donita as a Work In Progress

Profile of a Homeless Child 1990-1991

Having labored through much clinical data, this section will attempt to provide a vivid portrait of an actual homeless child. As meaningful as clinical data may be, to see the impact of homelessness on an individual may bring home more vividly the impact of homelessness than all the previous clinical data combined. What does homelessness look like and feel like through the eyes of one participant at Hopeful Horizons? This portrait is derived from a home visit, interview, and journal entries and is provided from two points in time. The first is an image of a child with great potential and the second is through the eyes of a person who has been forced to grow up far more rapidly with more hardship than four years should bring to any person.

Donita Kasey had a sad look in her eyes and an apathetic expression on her face as she explained to her teacher why her homework was incomplete. "If you lived in the environment that I lived in you'd know why." This 11-year-old female was definitely very bright and had an educational history of being placed in a "gifted and talented" program. If she had been attending any other school, she not only would have had homework but also enrichment activities to take home and complete each night. But now with all the changes in her life, she did well to concentrate on the day-to-day assignments while at school.

Donita lived with her mother and two siblings at the nearby shelter for battered women. When I entered the room on the second floor for the interview, it was apparent Donita's responsibilities were significant. She appeared at the door with a baby on her hip and a bottle in her hand. Her mother gave her instructions to take the kids downstairs. She soon returned asking if Josh had come back to the room, as she was unable to find him. The orders were to find him immediately before he got into trouble as he so often did, to which she responded by leaving the baby on the floor and beginning a search from room to room down the hall. The room was approximately 10' x 12' with a bathroom at the opposite end from the door. There was a regular sized bed and a cot, a dresser, a countertop next to a sink, no windows, and only dim lighting, but the floors were carpeted and the walls freshly painted. This was where the entire family had lived for three weeks. Her mother had brought them there to escape their stepfather's threats. Donita and her 6-year-old brother, Josh, had lived with their mother and father for five years. The parents divorced and Donita's father gained custody of the children for three years; however, he lost that right due to physical abuse and neglect. Donita and Josh came to live with their mother and stepfather, who had a son from a previous marriage, Kyle, now 21 years old. Her mother and stepfather then had a son, Jake, now 2 years old, and a daughter, Jessica, now 8 months old. They were living in the shelter because family life had become intolerable. Her mother had reported Kyle for sexual abuse of Josh. The stepfather was spending the family earnings on drugs refusing to pay the bills or to buy food.

During the interview, the mother had expressed her concern for Josh. He was failing kindergarten, acting out at Hopeful Horizons to the point they too were having a difficult time controlling him. She stated he would "hump" the younger son in an effort to display the sexual behavior he had learned from Kyle. Donita too was concerned about Josh; she watched him anxiously at school and was careful to defend him at any time necessary. When she was unable to attend school due to illness, she begged her mother not to let Josh go without her. When residential treatment was discussed for Josh, she became angry, although admitting she was aware he needed help.

Her mother seemed frustrated that Donita would not understand her position as she explained, "She puts me down and asks why I'd go back to him? She wants a T.V. mom and I just can't be that and never will. She's so smart and thinks that she can do it better, well she probably can but for now I'm the mom and I have to make the decisions that are best for me and the kids."

An Outside Perspective

At Hopeful Horizons, during interviews, the staff described Donita. She enjoys school and participates in the gifted and talented program; however, she is very depressed and isolates herself at times. Mom reports that she is angry with her. Donita reports happier days four years ago before her siblings were born and she became a surrogate mother.

Donita wrote in her journal: "This spring break I will do nothin, zip, zolach, as in suzulri, nothin. All I will do is go to the circus. This is nothing compared to everyone else's spring break. Spring break is not a good idea. Some of us have nothing to do, but sit and listen to our mothers."

Four Years Later

While walking down the hall of Hopeful Horizons, a young teen walked past and looked familiar. It was Donita Kasey, four years later again at Hopeful Horizons. What had happened? The social worker provided a history of the past four years. When Donita's mother left the shelter for battered women in 1991, she returned to her abusive husband. They struggled in and out of shelters and apartments, and the stepfather again battered Donita's mother. They had again moved to the shelter for abused women. The mother gave the stepfather the address, which for security reasons is never to be given out. The family was expelled from the shelter. They began the "shelter circuit;" in and out of several shelters. The mother was unable to protect the children and Donita was sexually molested; at what age and how often is unknown. The stepfather's involvement with drugs led to Donita having a drug dealer as a boyfriend. The mother kept Donita out of school to babysit the younger children.

This once "gifted and talented" child had grown into a sexually active, experienced surrogate mother, who was kept out of school to provide child care. While not studied explicitly, her life experience can be readily inferred and is not a pleasant sight with her stepfather, mother, and "drug dealing" boyfriend imposing custodial and sexual demands on a 15 year old adolescent who should be in school. That once nervous, sad, vulnerable look in her eyes was usurped by a "matter of fact, I know what life is all about" look. She had been robbed of her childhood and her innocence, and yet her teachers continued to describe her as a youth with great potential. She was helpful to others, intelligent, and well liked by peers as well as teachers and staff members. Her mother had continued on her own "narcissistic path," as described by the social worker. The mother needed help and Donita was supposed to be that help despite her own needs. The social worker described the interview with the mother as being similar to a taffy pull. She pulled in one direction trying to discuss Donita and the mother pulled in the opposite direction taking every opportunity to talk about herself. The mother arrogantly bragged about how intelligent she had been in school, naming honors and awards she had received.

Talking in a loud, flamboyant manner, she justified her exploitation of her children with a sense of entitlement. After several attempts to redirect the mother and an inability to arouse empathy from the mother for her daughter, the social worker thanked her for coming in and directed her to the door.

The Department of Human Services (DHS) became indirectly involved and began tracking the family. As more reports were filed of sexual abuse of the younger children, DHS became directly involved, and when a former perpetrator was allowed back in the home, DHS intervened and took the children from the mother. While at Hopeful Horizons, Donita had met with the social worker and said, "I want to live somewhere else even if it's foster care." During all this chaos, a young female counselor at the YWCA (Vicki) became friends with Donita. She was not Donita's counselor but had come to know her and several of the other youths through a program called Kids at Work. This program permitted Donita and others to follow a professional person around for a day to become familiar with that profession. Donita had become attached to this young professional. With Vicki working at the YWCA, she was easily accessible to Donita. When the difficulty with Donita's family intensified, she ran away from home, found out where Vicki lived, and showed up there, asking to stay. Vicki notified DHS and Donita was allowed to stay for two days. For the next few weeks, Vicki kept a close eye on what the court would do with this family and when the children were taken out of the home and put in foster care, Vicki petitioned the court to be the caregiver for Donita. The court agreed.

Two years have elapsed. Vicki continues to work with Donita, who has been involved as a candy striper at the Childrens' Hospital. It appears she has finally found the role model she desperately needed. At least that is our hope; that a Hopeful Horizon dawns each day for Donita.

References

Case histories are based on the developmental interviews. Identifying data (names and dates) have been changed to protect the individuals.

Balfour, R. (1991). "Teaching the homeless." *Thrust for Educational Leadership*, January, 30-32.

Bassuk, E.L. (1987). "The feminization of homelessness: families in Boston shelters." *American Journal of Social Psychiatry*, 7(1), 19-23.

Bassuk, E.L. & Gallagher, E. (1990). "The impact of homelessness on children." *Child and Youth Services*, 14(1), 19-33.

Bassuk, E.L. & Rosenberg L. (1990). "Psychosocial characteristics of homeless children and children with homes." *Pediatrics*, 85(3), March, 257-261.

Bassuk, E.L. & Rubin, L. (1987). "Homeless children: a neglected population." *American Journal of Orthopsychiatry*, 57(2), 279-86.

Bassuk, E.L., Rubin, L., & Lauriat, A.S. (1986). "Characteristics of sheltered homeless families." *American Journal of Public Health*, 76(9), 1097-1101.

Bender, L. (1946). "Instructions For the Use of Visual Motor Gestalt Test." The American Orthopsychiatric Association, Inc.

Biscoe, B. (1989). Program narrative. Education for Homeless Children and Youth (Catalog No. 84-225). Unpublished proposal, Oklahoma City Public School District, Oklahoma.

Blaine, G., Bergner, R., Lewis, M., & Goldstein, M. (1981). "The use of objectively scorable House-Tree-Person indicators to establish child abuse." *Journal of Clinical Psychology*, July, 37(3), 667-673.

Bogdan, R.C. & Biklen, S.K. (1982). Qualitative research for education: An introduction to theory and methods. Boston: Allyn and Bacon, Inc.

Bronfenbrenner, U. (1977). "Toward an experimental ecology of human development." *American Psychologist*, 32, 513-531.

Bronfenbrenner, U. (1979). The ecology of human development. United States of America: Harvard College.

Bronfenbrenner, U. (1986a). "Alienation and the four worlds of childhood." *Phi Delta Kappan*, 67, 430-436.

Bronfenbrenner, U. (1986b). "Ecology of the family as a context for human development: Research perspectives." *Developmental psychology*, 22(6), 723-742.

Burns, R.C. (1982). Self-growth in families kinetic family drawings (K-F-D) research and application. New York: Brunner Mazel Publishers.

Burns, R.C. & Kaufman, S. (1972). Actions, styles and symbols in kinetic family drawings (K-F-D). New York:Brunner Mazel Publishers.

Buros, O.K. (Ed.). (1965). The sixth mental measurements yearbook. Highland Park, New Jersey: The Gryphon Press.

Conoley, J.C. & Kramer, J.J. (Eds.). (1989). The tenth mental measurements yearbook. Lincoln, Nebraska: The University of Nebraska Press.

Eddowes, E. & Hranitz, J. (1989). "Educating children of the homeless." *Childhood Education*, Summer, 197-200.

Ely, L., et al. (1987, December). Broken lives: denial of to homeless children. (Report No. UD026010). Washington, D.C.: The National Coalition for the Homeless. (ERIC Document Reproduction Service No. ED 292897).

Erickson, F. (1984). "What makes school ethnography 'ethnographic'?" *Anthropology and Education Quarterly*, 15, 51-66.

First, P. & Cooper, G. (1989). "Access to education by homeless children." *West's Education Law Reporter*, 53(3), 757-65.

Fowler, R.D. (Ed.). (1991). "Homelessness [Special issue]." *American Psychologist*, 46(11).

Fox, E. & Roth, L. (1989). "Homeless children: Philadelphia as a case study." *The Annals of the American Academy*, 506, November, 141-149.

Fox, S., Barrnett, R., Davies, M., & Bird, H. (1990). "Psychopathology and developmental delay in homeless children: A pilot study." *Journal of the American Academy of Child and Adolescent Psychiatry*, 29(5), September, 732-735.

Gewirtzman, R. & Fodor, I. (1987). "The homeless child at school: from welfare hotel to classroom." *Child Welfare*, 516(3), 237-45.

Gonzalez, M. (1990). "School + home = a program for educating homeless students." *Phi Delta Kappan*, June, 785-87.

Goodman, L., Saxe, L., & Harvey, M. (1991). "Homelessness as psychological trauma." *American Psychologist*, 46(11), 1219-1225.

Hall, J. & Maza, P. (1990). "No fixed address: the effects of homelessness on families and children." *Child and Youth Services*, 14(1), 35-47.

Hamm, R.L. (1981). Philosophy and education. Danville, Illinois: The Interstate Printers & Publishers, Inc.

Harrington-Lueker, D. (1989a). "Sadly, Quinn's singular story is not unique." *The Executive Educator*, 11(12), December, 19.

Harrington-Lueker, D. (1989b). "What kind of school board member would help homeless children?" *The American School Board Journal*, July, 12-19.

Hartman, A. (1989). "Homelessness: public issue and private trouble." *Social Work*, November, 483-84.

"Homeless students get special school." (1990), November), *Tulsa Tribune*, 96 (281).

Horowitz, S., Springer, C., & Kose, G. (1988). "Stress in hotel children: The effects of homelessness on attitudes toward school." *Children's Environments Quarterly*, Spring, 5(1), 34-36.

Koppitz, E.M. (1963). The Bender Gestalt Test for Young Children Volume I. Boston: Allyn and Bacon.

Koppitz, E.M. (1975). The Bender Gestalt Test for Young Children Volume II Research and Application, 1963-1973. New York: Grune and Stratton, Inc.

Lauriat, A. (1986). "Sheltering homeless families: beyond an emergency response." *New Directions for Mental Health Services*, 30, 87-94.

Mills, C. & Ota, H. (1989). "Homeless women with minor children in the Detroit metropolitan area." *Social Work*, November, 485-89.

Mitchell, J.V. (Ed.). (1985). The ninth mental measurements yearbook. Lincoln, Nebraska: The University of Nebraska Press.

National Coalition for the Homeless (1989, May). Stewart B. McKinney Homeless Assistance Act Revised Summary (Report No. UD026809). Washington D.C.: The National Coalition for the Homeless. (ERIC Document Reproduction Service No. ED308264).

National Education Association Representative Assembly (1991, July). Bill of Rights for Children. Washington, D.C.: The National Education Association.

Newsletter of the National Coalition for the Homeless (1991, April). National Coalition for the Homeless, Washington, D.C.

Ogdon, D.P. (1986). Psychodiagnostics and personality assessment: a handbook. U.S.A.: Western Psychological Services.

Oklahoma State Department of Education (1989, December). Regional summary report of homeless children and youth served by shelters, Oklahoma City, Oklahoma: Department of Education, State of Oklahoma.

Penning, N. (1989). "Homeless Houston youth find refuge in schools." *The School Administrator*, 46(9), October, 23-25.

Perry, J. (1990). "Homeless children get chance to learn." *Daily Oklahoman*, November 26.

Piers, E.V. & Harris, D.B. (1969). Manual for the Piers-Harris Children's Self-Concept Scale. Nashville, Tennessee: Counselor Recordings and Tests.

Ploeg, J.D. van der, (1989). "Homelessness: a multidimensional problem." *Children and Youth Services Review*, 11, 45-56.

Quinn, T. (1989). "My hard encounter with the reality of homeless children." *The Executive Educator*, 11(12), December, 17-29.

Reigeluth, C.M. (Ed.). (1983). Instructional-design theories and models: An overview of their current status. Hillsdale, New Jersey: Laurence Erlbaum Associates, Publishers.

Reynolds, W.M. (1989). Reynolds Adolescent Depression Scale: Professional manual. Odessa, Florida: Psychological Assessment Resources.

Reynolds, W.M. (1989). Reynolds Child Depression Scale: Professional manual. Odessa, Florida: Psychological Assessment Resources.

Rivlin, L. (1990). "Home and homelessness in the lives of children." *Child and Youth Services*, 14(1), 5-17.

Rosenberg, Solarz, & Bailey. (1991). *American Psychologist.*

Rosenman, M. & Stein, M. (1990). "Homeless children: A new vulnerability." *Child and Youth Services*, 14(1), 89-109.

Seligman, M.E.P. (1975). Helplessness. San Francisco: W. H. Freeman and Company.

Shelly, P. (1988). "Between the rocks and hard places." *School Leader*, 17(7), September-October, 19-22.

"Shooting back." (1990, November), *Life*, 94, 95, 101.

Smith, L. (1991). "Positive Tomorrows offers educational alternative for children of city's homeless." *Oklahoma Gazette*, June 12.

Smith, L.M., Kleine, P.F., Prunty, J.P., and Dwyer, D.C. (1986). Educational innovators: Then and now. Brighton, England: Falmer Press.

State Plan for the education of homeless children and youth (1989, February). Oklahoma State Department of Education, Oklahoma City, Oklahoma.

Tesch, R. (1984). Phenomenological studies: a critical analysis of their nature and procedures. Paper presented at the annual convention of the American Educational Research Association, New Orleans, Louisiana.

Toro, P., Trickett, E., Wall, D., & Salem, D. (1991). "Homelessness in the United States." *American Psychologist*, 46(11), 1208-1218.

Tower, C. & White, D. (1989). Homeless students. West Haven, Connecticut: National Education Association Professional Library.

Wells, A. (1990). "Educating homeless children." *The Education Digest*, April, 30-33.

Whitman, B.Y., Accardo, P., Boyert, M., & Kendagor, R. (1990). "Homelessness and cognitive performance in children: a possible link." *Social Work*, 35(6), November, 516-519.

Wolcott, H.F. (1979). Study guide for ethnographic research methods in education. In R.M. Jaeger (Ed.), Alternative Methodologies in Educational Research (p. F1-F10). American Educational Research Association.

Index